# HOW TO RETIRE ON THE HOUSE

# HOW TO RETIRE ON THE HOUSE

## ANDREW JAMES McLEAN

CB
CONTEMPORARY
BOOKS
CHICAGO

**Library of Congress Cataloging-in-Publication Data**

McLean, Andrew James.
    How to retire on the house : seven great ways for using
your home to generate retirement $$$ / Andrew James
McLean.
        p.    cm.
    Includes index.
    ISBN 0-8092-4144-7 (paper) : $7.95 (FPT)
    1. Home equity conversion.    2. Mortgage loans,
Reverse.    3. Deeds of trust.    4. Housing, Single family—
Conversion to accessory apartments.    5. Retirement
income.    I. Title.
HG2040.45.M37    1990
332.024'01—dc20                                    90-44339
                                                        CIP

**Other books written by Andrew James McLean and published by Contemporary Books**

*Buying and Managing Residential Real Estate*

*Foreclosures: How to Profitably Invest in Distressed Real Estate*

*The Complete Guide to Real Estate Loans*

*Real Estate: The Ultimate Handbook*

*Making a Fortune Quickly in Fix-Up Properties*

Published by Contemporary Books, Inc.
180 North Michigan Avenue, Chicago, Illinois 60601
Manufactured in the United States of America
International Standard Book Number: 0-8092-4144-7

# Contents

# Preface

Are you aware that the estimated value of home equity retained by America's senior adults, 65 and older, is $750 billion? That's a huge amount of value. And it's obvious that many homeowners are equity-rich—but remarkably cash-poor.

Among other reasons, most of these equity-rich people got that way because of inflation, years of seemingly endless mortgage payments, and, generally, strong housing demand nationwide.

For most homeowners, this accumulated equity is their primary asset, perhaps more valuable than a company pension, if any, and likely more money than they could ever expect from Social Security—yet they cannot get at it. This equity, if properly utilized, can be a practical source of retirement income.

But how does one go about turning equity into income? You have several alternatives, and this book will carefully analyze the advantages of each:

- Sell the house outright, and receive all cash for your equity
- Sell the house on installment by accepting a down payment and carrying back an interest-bearing note from the buyers for the balance owing
- Rent out the home (which can include an option to buy)
- Take advantage of a reverse annuity mortgage, allowing you to receive a tax-free monthly sum on the equity in your home
- Refinance or take out a second mortgage loan
- Implement a sale-leaseback, which allows you to sell your house and continue to live in it by renting it back from the buyers
- Rent out an accessory room—the attic, a converted garage, or an extra bedroom, for example

However, before you implement any of these strategies, the disposition of the home you're living in deserves special attention. For instance, thinking like a homeowner, consider the following situations: How do you make the house worth thousands more (without spending a lot of money)? Which improvements pay, and which ones don't? And what about renting or buying a replacement home? If you buy, is it better to pay all cash or to finance the replacement home? What are the best tax strategies? Where might you retire to? And what are the best investment ideas for your money?

These and many other questions will be discussed on the following pages. Additional features include making the tax laws work for you, creating a multi-property estate, and financing your improvements. Following the last chapter is a special question-and-answer section about real estate, retirement, and income taxes, and a helpful glossary. Throughout the book, I endeavor to simplify what others tend to complicate.

This is not, however, a book of the "get rich quick" genre. Anyone expecting such results would be better off wagering at the race track.

No, the advice found within the pages of *How to Retire on the House* profiles real-life scenarios and probabilities. The guidelines and recommendations are based upon personal experience.

Quite simply, you have in your hands rules, suggestions, and guidelines written in a plainspoken, nontechnical style. Factoring in the best ways to make your home more valuable and how to get the most for it, you should find it easier to accomplish a comfortable retirement.

Whether you're a novice homemaker or a seasoned multiproperty landlord, you'll find this an excellent handbook covering a wide range of topics, advising you on the best ways to "retire on the house."

Best of luck for a happy and worry-free retirement.

# Acknowledgments

I would like to thank Howard Marcotte for his contri-
bution about how to invest in municipal bonds, Mark
Sheets for his clarification of the tax laws, and Ron
Marr, the syndicated columnist known as "The Word
Man," for his "Write Stuff" article.

# CHAPTER 1

# Introduction: In Search of Paradise

**Paradise:** A place of great contentment. A condition of great or perfect satisfaction, happiness, or delight.

—*Webster's New World Dictionary*, Third College Edition

More than anything else, humankind's endless love affair with the sea makes beachfront property eternally desirable. This is especially true along the sandy gulf coast beaches of southwest Florida, where you'll find a special kind of paradise.

Flourishing in a life-giving subtropical climate and situated along mangrove waterways skirting the Everglades lies Naples on the Gulf. Normally a charming town of little more than 60,000 inhabitants, it more than doubles in size when blustery winter weather sets in elsewhere.

During winter the tourists and snowbirds gradually migrate south, driven to the sun. Some pull up stakes and move, and some are just on vacation. Others take their houses with them, living in motor homes. After years in the north, most aging adults come to the realization that it's hard to be cold when you're old.

Far north of Florida, along the shores of Lake Superior and near the Canadian frontier, is Duluth, Minnesota. Duluth has the dubious distinction of being, according to the Census Bureau, the American city with the fastest-shrinking population (8 percent annually).

This, incidentally, corresponds to another little-known fact: International Falls, Minnesota, is on record as being, on average, the coldest American city. It is no coincidence that International Falls is only two hours down the road from Duluth.

## THE "BEST" OF THE BEST

It's also no coincidence that here in Naples, some of my friends are from Duluth. Of these transplanted Duluthians, my tennis-playing buddy Bob is the personification of "retiring on the house."

In 1980 Bob quit his job. He and his wife sold their house in Duluth and moved the family and furniture to Naples. They bought a beachfront condominium and began to enjoy a new and different lifestyle. After a year of getting accustomed to not working for someone else, Bob began to observe an interesting phenomenon. Up and down the gulf coast, a building boom was going on. Condominiums were springing up almost overnight, and they were sold before completion. Prices were going up too, sometimes 50 percent or more each year. Bob became confident that the demand for real estate, particularly beachfront land, would go on forever, as word of Naples's beauty and desirability swept the eastern half of the country.

During the next five years, Bob sold that original beachfront condo for a huge profit, and he bought and sold a dozen others. He also mentioned to me that his wife was tired of moving every six months. Regardless of his wife's dissatisfaction, he earned enough profits while buying and selling prime beachfront condos to pay $250,000 cash for the unit they now live in. That was three years ago. Today Bob says he wouldn't take half a million for it!

Bob owns and lives in what he calls "the best of the best." He claims that, by far, this unit is the most desirable in the entire condominium complex. Out of our hundred units, he occupies a second-floor corner unit with private beach access (a spiral staircase to ground level), one of only a pair with that feature in the entire project. Furthermore, because of being a corner unit, his condo has an extra screened patio with a view the other noncorner units don't have.

He found that, over the years, the best always appreciates the most. People who retire, especially if they have some money, want to live on the water. But most of the beachfront property has already been built on. Plenty of sites are available inland, but they are less desirable. In other words, the reason beachfront property is so valuable—the reason it increases proportionately more than other land—is that its supply is limited.

## THE "RETIRE ON THE HOUSE" FORMULA

Oddly enough, over a lifetime the house that made you equity-rich often becomes problematic, whether or not it is expensive. Over the years it appreciated in value, to perhaps two or three times or more what you paid for it. But when it's time to retire (or for that matter semiretire), that big, expensive house is burdensome. With escalating property taxes, lawns to mow, snow to shovel, and the kids gone, now is the time to convert that pent-up equity to income.

## The Formula in a Nutshell

Essentially, this book is about getting the most from what you already have. It's full of helpful advice and tips about how homeowners can profitably dispose of their house before or during retirement. It also shows how to retire worry-free. This includes how to wisely invest and a profile of special kinds of paradise you might consider retiring to—places like Las Vegas, southern California, and my particular favorite, Florida.

Here's the formula for retiring on the house:

1. Create maximum house value.
2. Convert your house value to retirement income.
3. Retire worry-free.
   • Shake the work habit.
   • Know what to look for in a retirement home.
   • Wisely invest what you have.

I'll show you what you need to know.

## RETIRING "ON THE HOUSE" TAKES LESS MONEY THAN YOU THINK

During the working years, you need more income than you do after retirement because you're usually supporting children, a big house, and all the expenses that go along with them. You probably own more than one car, a recreational vehicle or two, perhaps a boat, and you have to spend money on business lunches, commuting, and work clothes.

But when you're retired, either you don't have or don't need these things. By then the kids are probably living in a home of their own, and because you're not working, you don't need a second car or a business wardrobe. On average, most people can retire comfortably on two-thirds of the money they lived on during their working years.

## How Much Money Do You Need?

Most financial planners agree that you need a net worth of at least $400,000 to retire comfortably. That's total net worth, including home equity, pension funds, and vehicles. If you convert that amount of net worth to cash and put it in CDs, you'll earn about 8 percent, yielding a pretax annual income of $32,000. (That's more than what 65 percent of American working families make.) Interest rates are always changing, so your income could be slightly more or less, but that kind of money should be an adequate retirement income.

Of course, it's possible to retire on a net worth of as little as $200,000, but that's really pulling the purse strings tight. At 8 percent, that computes to a pretax income of $16,000 annually. On that amount, you'd have to be willing to make certain sacrifices. After a few years of retirement, you may want to unretire and take on a part-time job until you qualify for Social Security.

## Retiring on $60 a Day

Financial planners estimate that retiring on $60 a day is a reasonable goal to plan for. Of course, living on $60 a day requires a few conditions. It presumes that you're not supporting children, the in-laws, or your parents. And $60 a day won't go very far in places like New York City or Paris. Realistically, it assumes you'll be retiring in the more popular and inexpensive sites around the United States, such as Florida or Arizona.

The $60-a-day rule says that you spend $60 a day on you, not on your assets. That's $21,900 a year. Right now you're probably spending more than that. If you're like most Americans, the more you make, the more you spend. The interest alone on an American household's portfolio of charge cards could probably support a small town in Poland. Then each year on April 15, Uncle Sam takes his share, fair or otherwise.

In short, after paying to maintain national security—and after paying for the freedom to live in a capitalistic society where you can make all that money—your hard-earned income goes to sustain your assets.

I know, because I've been there. I like to refer to it as "assetitis." It's a disease of the working class. It means working for your assets, instead of your assets working for you. Non-income-producing assets, like a big house and flashy car, produce expenses. When you retire, you'll find it's better to have your equity in liquid assets that work for you. You do this by trading down that big, expensive house and replacing it with an affordable home.

## HOW I DID IT

I have spent the better part of the last 20 years purchasing, restoring, and then selling for a profit the homes I lived in. I didn't inherit a fortune, win a lottery, outguess the stock market, or beat the tables in Las Vegas. I wasn't a millionaire. But I did have some savings and equity in my home and in several income properties. I simply wanted a life of my own, away from the bosses—not a job where someone else capitalized on my time and effort.

Along the path to glory, we occasionally step on a

few land mines. Most of us, being the fallible humans we are, make mistakes along the way. Yet it's the wise person who learns from his or her mistakes.

Twenty years of buying and selling houses didn't always produce profits. Sometimes I sold at a loss; at times I paid too much, and a few times I was ripped off. Although I didn't always do it right, I did learn from my mistakes. And this firsthand experience is yours for the taking.

# CHAPTER 2

# Improvements and Increasing Value: Making the Home Worth More

Most people think of their house as a shelter from the bustling outside world or simply as a place to live—the place where they eat, entertain, play, love, and come in from harsh weather. But your house is much more than a roof over your head and a place to reside. If you're like most homeowners, your house is likely your prime asset—the biggest investment you ever made. And with little exception, your house has substantially appreciated over the years of owning it.

Regardless of its value now, with a minimum of effort and expenditure, your house can be worth much more, perhaps thousands more. To accomplish this, you must treat your prime asset as the investment it truly is.

## LEARN FROM THE PROS

All that's required is that you become educated in the skills of the home improvement game—savvy taken from professional renovators, decorators, landscape architects, Realtors, people who know, experts who've done it. As a professional renovator over the last 20 years, I have made it my business to buy, renovate, and resell residential real estate at a profit. In this chapter, I endeavor to pass on to you the benefits of my expertise as well as the know-how of other professionals and experts.

You're going to learn why certain houses increase in value and why others do not. You'll learn how to make your house more marketable and how you can make it increase in value faster than you ever thought possible. You'll also learn which improvements add the most value. And you'll learn methods for making your house more desirable to the majority of potential home buyers. Finally, you'll learn how to economically create new living space that will add value to your home. In doing so, you'll create a house that few potential home buyers can say no to.

I've learned, as have most professional renovators, that there are a variety of simple improvements you can make that will increase the value of your home much more than the cost of those improvements. For instance, it's possible to add desirability as well as $3,000 in market value to your home simply by planting $600 in landscaping. You can even create visual or aesthetic improvements, all with proportionately small expenditures of money and labor.

Take, for example, a home I purchased several years ago in Las Vegas. It was a custom ranch home on a half-acre of horse-zoned land. Although this home was extremely well built and functional, it lacked visual appeal. It had no character or style; from a visual point of view, it was just too plain and simple. For example, when people first entered the home from the foyer, they were confronted with a large sunken living room. This area was carpeted wall to wall, and the carpeting extended up the interior walls about 12 inches—sort of a carpet baseboard.

Somehow I knew, from the first day I discovered that eyesore, that all it needed was a few minor renovations to make it more desirable. For starters, both the carpet and the carpet baseboard had to go. In its place I visualized oak planking with oak baseboards. That carpet was the primary visual deterrent of what otherwise was a beautiful home. And except for the kitchen cabinets, the house lacked any natural wood whatsoever. Everything was paint and carpet.

For the time being, I left the carpet intact, leaving the living room temporarily as it was, made other minor renovations, and put the house up for sale. While observing prospective buyers as they inspected the house, I noticed that they were not pleased with the living room. So, after a month of unsuccessfully trying to sell the house, I took it off the market.

Immediately I pulled up the living room carpet and carpet baseboards, then installed solid oak planking. In addition, I paneled the foyer with solid oak stained the color of the new wood floor. The whole job cost about $1,200. Without being overly modest, I must say it was gorgeous. The added warmth exuded by the stained wood enhanced the beauty of this home. With the flooring complete, I put the house up for sale and added $15,000 to the asking price. Within two weeks I had sold the house at full price.

As you can see, just the alteration of one room not only earned over 12 times my investment, but it also was the primary reason this particular house sold so fast.

To make your house worth thousands more while profiting from the improvements you've made, you must follow these guidelines:

- Upgrade your home according to what potential home buyers are looking for.
- Give your home a style that appeals to your taste as well as that of most potential home buyers.

## YOUR HOUSE IS ONLY AN OBJECT IN THE MARKETPLACE

No matter how much you may adore your house, you must learn to envision it as an object in the marketplace. Your house may figure prominently in your dreams or feelings of security, but the fact remains that it is a thing of greater or lesser value in the overall housing marketplace. Different as your home may be, buyers will be comparing it in value with other available homes.

Therefore, the price of your home depends on all the features and amenities that buyers in the market deem important—not what you, individually, feel is important. For instance, you may believe that a gazebo in the backyard is worth $2,000. But to a potential home buyer who is not interested in a gazebo, it's worthless. Or, a $10,000 swimming pool in the backyard of a home in Duluth, Minnesota, might pose a similar problem. On the other hand, today's buyers are looking for features like fireplaces, a family room, more than one bathroom, a laundry room, and patios or decks—and they are willing to pay for them.

Once you envision your home merely as an object in the marketplace, it will become clear to you how to make it worth the most for the least expenditure. Nevertheless, many homeowners make the mistake of doing inappropriate improvements—ones that may satisfy their own needs and not the needs of the marketplace. They don't begin thinking of the marketplace until it's time to sell, and then it's too late.

Now is the time, while you're still living in your home, to start thinking of it as an object in the marketplace, not later when you may have done irreparable harm to your prime asset. Perhaps the most damaging notion is that you perceive your home as your castle, and that you can alter it according to what you like.

A friend of mine in Michigan—we'll call him Jim—is a wealthy and successful trial attorney with more wisdom and education than Carter has liver pills. However, he lacks sound judgment when it comes to investing in his home. Jim often asked my advice on expensive renovations to his newly acquired home; unfortunately, he never took my advice seriously.

Jim purchased a classic colonial house in a quaint section of Detroit. With six bedrooms and four bathrooms, including 4,000 square feet of living space, it was not considered a mansion or an estate but accurately could be described as a big period house in better-than-average condition. Against my advice, he proceeded to alter this classic house into a contemporary yuppie pad. Besides the $195,000 he paid for the house, he invested another $90,000 in renovations. (Most buyers would have been satisfied to live in the house "as is.")

First Jim had the natural oak trim and baseboards painted throughout the entire house. (The wood was not in the best of condition, but it could have been stripped and refinished.) Then he ordered the contractor to cover the ornamental ceiling plasterwork with sheetrock. He also ordered new carpeting for the living and dining rooms to hide the worn oak planking. (He should have refinished the planking and bought a few area rugs.)

Next he had the kitchen overhauled, using a design that matched, to a T, page 17 of the November issue of *Architectural Digest*. (That kitchen was designed for a sunny southern California beach home, with fluorescent lighting and a skylight.) In addition, he had an exotic swimming pool built, complete with an adjacent Jacuzzi and redwood changing room.

Finally, as if all this weren't enough, he decided on a gaudy wallpaper design to decorate the guest bedrooms. (I would call it "contemporary Red Roof Inn".)

As you can see, in extreme form, Jim transformed this classic period house into his own fantasy home. He made alterations and so-called improvements without considering the wants of future buyers. Yuppie-type extra features might be nice for a few, but the majority of potential home buyers won't pay for them. It's highly unlikely Jim will ever recoup the additional $90,000 he invested in these inappropriate renovations.

Of course, there is a remote possibility that someone, somewhere, with eccentric tastes similar to Jim's, would find this so-called quasi-contemporary colonial house desirable and be willing to pay what Jim has invested in it. But we, as investors, don't want the possible; we want the probable. An essential principle of basic value states, *Homeowners are much more likely to get a better price for their house if it appeals to a large number of buyers, instead of to a rare individual.* Picture your house in a housing auction: the more buyers that bid on it, the greater the price.

As a thing of value in the marketplace, a house will be valued at its greatest worth when it's basically conventional (appeals to the greatest number of buyers) and has relatively few amenities or features that make it stand out against other, similarly conventional houses. It's common knowledge that home buyers want a house that's tastefully decorated, well constructed, in good condition, and a little different. They will pay a premium to get these things.

In other words, for the investment-minded renovator, the house need not appeal to a few eccentrics, but it should appeal to the greatest possible number of buyers who will be interested in that kind of house. Regarding Jim's house, I can't think of many people who'd want fluorescent lighting and covered-over oak floors (not to mention the pool and Jacuzzi in such a cold climate) in a classic French colonial.

## WHAT BUYERS WANT

According to a survey conducted by National Family Opinion Corp., home buyers say they want bigger houses and yards, even if it means giving up some expensive extras. The survey also concluded that "buyers will purchase a well-designed smaller house that makes good use of the space available."

The survey of 814 house seekers found that home buyers are spending more time at home and want plenty of room to spend it in. More than 85 percent said they are staying home more often; only 14.5 percent said they spend most of their free time elsewhere. Seventy percent of the house hunters said they want at least two bathrooms, and 48 percent desired an oversized master bathroom.

Other findings:

- Nearly 80 percent want a full basement.
- More than 50 percent want three bedrooms.
- Nearly 57 percent want a separate dining room.
- More than 45 percent want a two-car garage.

Additionally, the survey noted that home buyers are looking for more storage area, kitchen with eating place, larger family rooms, and larger closets. It also said that porches and patios remain popular among home buyers.

## PLANNING THE RENOVATIONS

Making improvements to your house and at the same time gaining the most value from them just doesn't happen without thoughtful planning. If you want to recoup proportionately more than you invest in renovations, then the alterations you make must be carefully thought out.

Sooner or later the time to sell your home will come. Change, like death and taxes, is inevitable. You may retire to a warmer climate. You may have to relocate out of town because of a job change. Your spouse dies. Your kids move away to college. Whatever the reason, according to statistics the average owner-occupied home in this country sells every seven years (every five years in the western states).

Ideally, then, you want to take full advantage of the effects of inflation on your investment in renovations. You accomplish this by planning now for gains that will be made later.

You can put the investment odds in your favor by analyzing the overall housing marketplace, then making the appropriate lowest-cost renovations that appeal to the greatest number of buyers. By shrewdly planning your home improvements, you can be assured that over the long term you can expect an outstanding rate of return on your investment. This is primarily due to inflation and to satisfying the buyer's demand in the housing marketplace.

Inflation not only increases the overall value of your

renovated house each year; it also increases the value of each improvement you've made. This increase in value is the result of the ever-increasing costs of labor and material. Today's brick fireplace valued at $1,200 will be worth $2,400 in seven years, and buyers will pay for it. At the same time, you can enjoy the greater beauty, space, pride of ownership, and more functional home that the improvement offers.

## HOUSE STYLE

Remember the Las Vegas house I mentioned earlier? It was a well-cared-for and functional home, but until I added the natural wood enhancements, it lacked style. Before the appropriate alterations were made, the home was too plain. Prospective buyers just walked through it without interest. After the alterations were made, prospective buyers stopped at the foyer and delighted in the woodwork. I could see them imagining themselves living in this stylish home.

Style in a home is an effect, a feeling, an image. Perhaps it's the beautiful oak mantel over the fieldstone fireplace, or the hardwood floors that give the home a special effect. It could be the furnishings, in which colors and textures blend together harmoniously to capture an aesthetic style.

A house with style is not only pleasing and stimulating to live in, but it will also sell faster and get a better price than its unstylish neighbor. Home buyers are looking for style. They want something special, out of the ordinary—something that exudes personal charm when they entertain friends and relatives. Buyers want to feel that the house they purchase has a personality, especially after they've made the down payment and committed themselves to a costly long-term mortgage.

Style is an intangible asset and doesn't necessarily

cost a great deal to create. Even a small, inexpensive home can have aesthetic style. On the other hand, a mansion valued at $1 million can lack definable style.

You can learn to develop a sensitivity to style. It originates in the mind and evolves out of the innovative and creative skills of the homeowner.

Your home is the mirror image of your soul. It transcends a description of who you are. Your home reveals to everyone entering it who you are—more so than the clothes you wear, your occupation, or the friends you have.

The house you live in reveals how you live. People entering your abode for the first time, naturally curious as humans are, will get certain clues about you. To a greater or lesser degree, your house reveals a lifestyle, including whether you're a neat or sloppy housekeeper, where the kids eat, where the animals are fed, who smokes in the family, and the size of your wardrobe.

Human nature is such that we care what other people think about our lifestyle. Consequently, we care what our home—its warmth, the serenity of the overall environment, its decor, and order—says about us. All of this is a portrait of who we are, and as difficult as it is to describe, it's the heart and soul of that profitable and desirable concept of house style.

## THE HOUSE WITHOUT STYLE

The house without style is dull and indefinable. It may be in a good location, solidly constructed and functional, but without certain niceties it won't be special or unique. The house that lacks style has nothing to distinguish it from all the other houses on the block. The house without style lacks certain features and amenities, the carefully thought-out conveniences—

wet bar, fireplace, mirrored walk-in closets, separate laundry room—that make us feel distinguished and add a kind of status to the home.

Such a run-of-the-mill house—ordinary, dull, un-distinguished—will undoubtedly capture the lowest possible price for similar homes in the marketplace. Should you own such a house, it's still possible to make a small profit on it because inflation will eventually increase the value somewhat. Conversely, if you add a certain style even to the most conventional and ordinary four-walled structure, you can be assured the value will increase accordingly.

## HOW TO CREATE STYLE

Essentially, there are three basic rules in the art of creating style in a house: give it a theme, keep it simple, and add features.

### Giving Your House a Theme

Creating a theme is very important to giving your house a certain style. This is because it allows you to get a handle on what renovations will enhance or detract from the style you're trying to create. Developing a theme assists you in creating a certain ambience, look, or image to your home.

For instance, let's say your house belongs to a certain architectural era, such as Victorian, Tudor, or Gothic. If this is the case, then by all means stay with the look that's already been established. You can work wonders accentuating, say, the simplicity of a Cape Cod or an old midwestern farmhouse. If you own a Victorian or English Tudor home, consider doing some research at the library so you can authenticate the decor. At the same time, you'll want to modernize;

however, it's important to retain the nostalgic charm of the original look.

Keep in mind that people in today's synthetic culture crave antiquity. They want to be a part of history. They want roots. By offering them a certain amount of nostalgia, you not only gain by the greater demand for your house, you also get to enjoy these features while you're living in it.

If your house does not belong to a noteworthy architectural period, then there are other methods of developing a theme for it. To accomplish this, you have to clearly think about the function of the house. To help yourself focus on the subject, ask who and what the house is for. If it's a family house, how many are in the family? Is the home for newlyweds or retirees? Is it a second vacation house or a permanent country home? Will it be used for solitude and creative work, or will guests be entertained there?

When you carefully think about the function of the house (and about its function for potential buyers), it's easier to conceptualize sensible renovations. The following examples illustrate how function in a country home can serve as the basis for style: If the house will be used in winter, you may want to make initial renovations to provide features that keep heating costs down. Think about ease of maintenance; family or guests who use the house only on weekends want to keep cleaning to a minimum. To most weekend vacationers, luxurious surroundings are less important than serenity and a beautiful view. Thus, elaborate bathrooms or large walk-in closets would not be necessary; a fireplace or wood-burning potbellied stove would be. In the kitchen, it's best to keep it simple, providing that you have an adequate supply of electricity for modern appliances and the needs of potential buyers.

Besides the function of the home, you have to think of decor. When I think of a charming country home, certain items come to mind as being appropriate, while other things are unsuitable. Rattan or ultra-modern furniture would certainly be out of place in a weekend country home, yet Early American antiques would likely do just fine. Maintenance-free floors are a must. A no-wax vinyl is OK, but polyurethaned wood is nicer. So is Spanish tile (in the western United States) or fieldstone. Furniture doesn't have to be elaborate, but it should be comfortable—large slip-covered couches (or convertible couches if you have a large family or expect numerous guests), a large wood dining table, and a few washable rugs. Complement all this with a few wooden benches for decorative pots, magazines, and plants. What more do you need in simple country comforts besides a warm crackling fire in the winter or cool breezes in the summer?

The fact of the matter is that theme sells. It will not only give your house order, it gives a distinct flavor and charm that sets it apart from other indefinable houses on the block. Furthermore, as mentioned earlier, creating a theme sets certain guidelines, enabling you to get a handle on the renovations that add style to your house.

## Keeping It Simple

The second rule, *keep it simple,* is relevant to improvements and to the decor of the house. Essentially it means avoiding the overly impressive look that will turn off or disturb potential buyers. This look includes excessive or artificial ornamentation, gaudy or distasteful paint on the walls, and bizarre lighting schemes. Such artifice does more to detract from the style of the house than to enhance it.

Use authentic materials that will endure over the years. Instead of plastic tile in the bathrooms, use genuine ceramic tile. Instead of synthetic wood flooring, use good cuts of hardwood. And for kitchen and bath appliances, install the simplest no-frills models from reputable manufacturers. The materials you use don't have to be the best money can buy. They do, however, have to be authentic. In our plasticized culture, authenticity becomes more valuable every day.

This brings to mind another restoration project I did several years ago in Las Vegas. I purchased an older ranch house with a spacious family room that had been converted from a three-car garage. The entire room, including beamed ceiling and a three-sided fireplace that extended out from an exterior wall, had been sprayed in white paint. To correct this hideous condition, I made some simple alterations. First, I painted the ceiling beams dark brown, which nicely accentuated the ceiling. Second, I built a natural oak mantel along the three faces of the fireplace. The whole job cost less than $50. And these two simple alterations changed a garish family room into a beautiful one. (I could have sand-blasted the paint off the brick on the fireplace, but I decided against that because it would be expensive and messy.)

Keeping it simple also means maintaining a clean ambience about your house. Visually, the lines of your house and outbuildings (garage, storage shed, pool house) should be kept clean and uncluttered. Store all the unnecessary stuff away, and repair things that are visually disruptive (such as a broken antenna or the kid's dilapidated tree house). When buyers approach your property, they should be presented with an overall pleasing view, one where the outbuildings and landscaping are in harmony with the focal point of the scene: the house.

## Adding Features

The third rule is to add features that help create style, and inevitably greater value, to your house. Well-conceived amenities (instead of money-wasting extras) will make your house special, unique, more functional than the ordinary house. Moreover, features add status to a house and will make potential buyers feel they're getting something special.

Features mean added convenience and function, things you're able to do or enjoy that you couldn't before the feature was there. Examples of added features are an extra family room with fireplace, an added redwood deck, or a built-in microwave oven. These are all things that you (and later owners) can enjoy and that make the house more functional.

Features stimulate the imagination. Ad writers frequently use them to stimulate the readers' so-called hot buttons. For example, house listings have touted the following features: "Sauna bath in master suite," "Walnut-paneled library," "Large yard with fruit trees." These ads were written to motivate the reader to imagine a rich and comfortable life.

People want special features and modern conveniences, will look for them, and will pay a premium, in excess of what the features cost, for the houses that have them. Keep in mind, however, that some people will pay for an extra bathroom, whereas few will pay for a sauna.

Certain features are considered more in demand to potential buyers and add more value to your house than the cost to make them. The special features considered most in demand by contemporary house hunters include an extra room, a master suite, an extra bathroom, a patio or deck, attractive landscaping, a laundry area, and certain kitchen conveniences. The features recommended here are based on the combined knowledge taken from a nationwide study of Realtors, builder's trade journals, and my own experience and that of other professional renovators.

## Extra Room

The addition of an extra room—one that can be used as a guest bedroom, den, family room, library, or combination of all of these—is a real plus. People need a special room in which to be solitary at times. Parents especially may need a place to get away from the kids and pursue a hobby or do some work without being disturbed. Depending on the interests of the homeowners, such a room could be set up as a sewing room, workshop, or office. But generally studies have shown that, throughout the country, most buyers want one extra room that can function as a den/family room or a guest bedroom.

## Master Suite

The master suite is a large bedroom set off from the rest of the house, preferably with its own bathroom and dressing area. A genuine, first-rate master suite will have such features as a fireplace, sliding glass doors leading to outdoor living areas (patio or deck), and large, mirrored walk-in closets. Today's house buyers are showing tremendous interest in having a master suite. They're looking for a feeling of warmth and privacy, a kind of combination bedroom and secluded living room. Noted builders have compiled hints about special features that people want in a master suite:

● Create a feeling of warmth and style with a fireplace.

- Connect the room to secluded outdoor living areas.
- Add a sense of the rich life with an opulent bath.
- Emphasize spaciousness with a large walk-in closet and dressing area.
- When space is not available, accentuate elegance by stressing architecture.

## Extra Bathroom

In a house with three bedrooms or more, an extra bathroom is an absolute must. Any family that requires three bedrooms or more will, no doubt, be grateful for the extra bath. For that reason alone, they will prefer a house that has an extra bathroom over a similar house without one.

There are, however, alternatives to this feature. You could create a half bath (a toilet and a sink) or a three-quarter bath (a half bath plus a shower but no tub) instead of a full bath, if the one bath in the house is adequate. You could expand the usability of the existing bathroom by adding a lavatory (sink) and dressing area. Many young first-time home buyers, for example, are content as long as they have two lavatories. Sometimes, especially due to lack of space, you might consider adding a half bath instead of a second full bath. Quite often you can simply add a shower stall and toilet to the master bedroom. Or a toilet and sink can be installed in the master bedroom, adding great convenience to a home.

When considering the added feature of a full bath or any of its components, careful planning is very important. Avoid making such an installation a major construction project unless your house is already worth a lot of money. Install the extra half bathroom under a stairway, in the corner of the master bedroom, or at the back of the house where it can tie in to the existing plumbing.

## Patios and Decks

Extending the casual living area to the outdoors not only makes your home more functional; if done properly, it can enhance the visual appeal as well as the value of your home. You can actually double or triple the investment value when you keep it simple. Use only weather- and insect-proof materials, while at the same time maintaining a pleasing proportion to the house itself. Patios and decks should also be located and landscaped for privacy. A redwood deck along with a barbecue and clay planters, especially if they overlook a great view, will accentuate any housing plan.

The more you invest in outdoor amenities, whether they include an enclosed patio or redwood deck or brick barbecue, the less likely you'll be to recoup the investment. Keep your outdoor improvements simple yet imaginative and practical.

## Landscaping

Blossoming flora and special landscaping will enhance the ambience surrounding even the blandest looking house. Although growing lush gardens may not bring a favorable return on money and labor invested, it's a very helpful feature in marketing your home. You need mature landscaping to grace the exterior features of your house. Nothing will more readily lure prospective buyers out of their cars than well-kept trees and shrubs and a manicured lawn. In fact, a healthy-looking and well-maintained lawn is a good index of how the overall property has been maintained and establishes that vital first impression. According to the United States Forest Service, well-landscaped homes with trees that are well kept bring an average of 15 percent more on resale.

Most landscaping reaches its prime value eight to twelve years after planting. Because of this, you should immediately invest in landscaping if your property needs it or if the landscaping you have lacks visual appeal. If you think there will be enough time for landscaping to mature, then by all means invest in the cheaper and less mature plants and shrubs. If, however, you lack the normal required growing time, it's better to purchase more mature landscaping. Five-year-old shrubs, for instance, are about half their normal mature size and are big enough not to look skimpy.

The following are some basic principles of landscaping:

- Use ivy or shrubbery to hide an unsightly or exposed foundation.
- Use vines or ivy to screen eyesores on your property or a neighboring property.
- Use landscaping to create privacy.

## Laundry Area

A laundry area is a convenience appreciated by everyone, especially a large family. If space permits, be sure to provide shelves for laundry supplies and a place to sort and hang large quantities of clothing. You can also use louvered bifold doors to conceal the laundry area.

Most people like the laundry area to be located inside or adjacent to the kitchen. The basement is a popular alternative to make use of wasted space and to inexpensively tie in to existing plumbing. For the finishing touch, don't forget adequate lighting.

## Kitchen Conveniences

Whatever you can add in features that create order and convenience in the kitchen will inevitably pay a bonus. Surveys have found that, if space permits, a separate eating area or center work island (peninsula) is what buyers are looking for. (A center work island with plenty of storage space is a very attractive feature.) Buyers are also looking for a self-cleaning or built-in microwave oven.

Buyers will not, however, pay for such decorative items as French baker's racks, track lighting, or top-of-the-line hardwood cabinets.

Buyers are also looking for plenty of storage space in the kitchen. In addition, consider the natural light-enhancing feature of a skylight. It provides the extra bonus of a life-giving effect on plants.


# PAINTING THE EXTERIOR

More often than not, you don't necessarily have to paint the entire exterior of the house before selling it. Unless the old paint is worn and peeling all over, you're actually better off just touching up the bad spots and painting the trim.

If the house does require a complete paint job, the color you choose can actually give an illusion of size. Picture, if you will, a light tan, one-story house in the high desert of Las Vegas, Nevada. The landscape surrounding the structure is sparse with vegetation, perhaps a tree or two and a few cabbage palms. And the flat, sandy ground is similar in color to the house. Now, if we paint that house with a vivid color (red, blue, or dark green), can you imagine what happens to the visual effect? The house stands out from its surroundings like a fish out of water, and it looks considerably smaller. A prospective buyer would probably pass it by, thinking that the house looks inappropriate or that it's too small for the family.

Along the same line of thinking, contrasting trim on a house will almost always make it appear smaller. If your house is big and harmoniously proportioned, yet lacking structural detailing, contrasting trim may add character. But if you're attempting to create a larger look, stay with a single color.

Remember that people, in general, are conventional. They prefer conventional colors—white, off-white, or tan—over vivid or extraordinary colors. As a rule, then, the brighter or more unconventional the exterior color of the house, the fewer potential buyers will be attracted to it.

## INTERIOR WALLS

Nothing turns off prospective buyers more than dirty, cracked, or water-damaged walls. Sometimes all that's necessary to make the walls clean and bright is cleaner and a wet sponge. But if your house has been lived in for a while, you'll probably need more than tidying up and spackling to patch the holes.

If the walls in your house are in poor condition—deteriorated plaster, gashes, or large sections of damaged wallboard—you can often make substantial changes or do the repairs yourself. The following are a few cost-saving suggestions for wall coverings that will appeal to the majority of prospective buyers:

● Give texture to an uneven wall or ceiling by adding sand to the paint. This will not only hide the flawed unevenness, but will also create an appealing surface.

● Use a less expensive vinyl-coated wallpaper instead of a pure vinyl paper in the kitchen and bathrooms. Apply over it a coat of low-gloss polyurethane, which protects the paper and makes it stain-resistant and scrubbable.

● Cover a badly cracked wall with old barn siding. Assuming that you can locate an old barn and remove the old boards with the owner's permission, your only expense will be the cost of transportation, glue, nails, and furring strips.

As with the exterior, for the house to appeal to the greatest number of buyers, the color of the interior walls should be neutral. Tan, beige, or antique white blend with any furniture scheme. Unfortunately, buyers will reject a perfectly suitable house if their furnishings clash with a garishly painted room.

Remember that buyers are looking for larger houses. Ultimately then, you should make it your objective to have the rooms in your house appear as large as possible. If more space seems available, the buyer is apt to pay more. Color plays a significant role in how the human eye visualizes the size of a room. The following tips describe how the use of color will visually enhance the size of rooms:

● Pale, whitish colors reflect light and should be used to make a room appear larger than it is.

● Light-colored ceilings appear higher; dark-colored ceilings appear lower.

● Vertically striped wallpaper visually heightens a room.

● Large or busy prints—wallpapers that have a lot of designs, lines, and contrasting colors—can make a room appear smaller. Wall coverings that have small prints with little contrast can make a room seem larger.

# CEILINGS

Uneven, cracked, or stained ceilings detract from what would otherwise be an attractive house. As most houses grow older, natural settling occurs, causing cracks and sags. Depending on the amount of damage, you have the option of either patching the damaged ceiling or replacing it with a new one.

Installation of a suspended ceiling can conceal a range of problems, from ceiling sags to unevenness and water damage (assuming the leak has already been repaired). Ceiling tiles or panels are simply suspended from the old ceiling on a metal grid, or they can be glued or stapled to furring strips.

Uneven or water-stained ceilings can be textured over with a sand-and-paint mixture. This option has several advantages: it's easy to apply, inexpensive, and very appealing. To prevent water stains from showing through, cover the stain with two coats of pigmented shellac as a sealer before applying the sand-and-paint mixture.

Don't forget to provide air vents or fans to promote the circulation of rising warm air for comfort in hot weather. Also, consider installing a skylight in an appropriate room. A skylight facing south will add light to an otherwise dreary room, give life to plants, and provide solar heat in the winter.

# FLOORS

Restoring floors to a clean and bright condition is imperative before selling the house. That's because the floor is the first thing most buyers look at when they enter the house. Flooring provides a feeling of solidity, and its color and brightness contribute to visual pleasure as well as enhancing the overall ambience of the house.

Restoring the surface of floors, whether they be wood, vinyl, linoleum, ceramic, or masonry, isn't that difficult. The following are helpful ideas and techniques for quick and economical floor improvement.

## Wood Floors

Most people prefer hardwood floors to plywood and carpet. A badly worn carpet will affect the amount of the offer that is made and the time it takes to sell the house. If your carpet covers a hardwood floor and is showing signs of wear, consider removing the carpet and restoring the floor. The first thing a buyer thinks about when he or she sees a worn-out carpet is how much replacing it will cost.

Wax buildup discolors a floor and makes it look dirty when it isn't. If your floors are in this condition, buyers are likely to think the floors actually need replacing—at their expense. The best way to remove old layers of acrylic or wax is to use good old elbow grease and number 2 steel wool. Wax removers will soften the hardened layers and make the scrubbing easier. Once the layers are removed, apply a coat of polyurethane. It's very durable and virtually maintenance-free. Polyurethane doesn't need waxing, and a damp sponge is all that's needed to remove dirt and restore the floor to its original luster.

## Vinyl Floors

Inlaid vinyl is a resilient type of flooring and is predominantly in use today. It may be of the no-wax variety or could have a factory-applied sealer, which eventually will wear off. The type with factory-applied sealer should only be coated with special sealers recommended by the manufacturer (not with shellac, lacquer, or varnish). On the other hand, a no-wax floor can be waxed with a self-polishing product once it becomes dull.

## Composition Tile Floors

Made from resinous fibers, composition tile is found in many older homes. Like vinyl, it should not be coated with shellac, lacquer, or varnish. After removing the old polish, apply a self-polishing wax. Do not use oil or liquid polishing wax, paste wax, strong detergents, or chemicals.

## Linoleum Floors

If your linoleum floor has become worn and discolored, strip off the old wax, then coat it with a good deck or floor enamel and a subsequent coat of self-polishing wax. Avoid using scouring powders and harsh detergents, which will damage linoleum's sealed surface. As with vinyl floors, coatings of shellac, lacquer, or varnish will damage linoleum and should never be used.

## Masonry Floors

Masonry floors—including stone, slate, terrazzo, tile, and marble—are durable and virtually maintenance-free. If masonry floors are not already sealed, first use bleach to clean the grout, then apply an acrylic sealer. Apply a polishing or self-polishing wax for additional protection.

Clean an unpainted cement floor with four table-spoons of trisodium phosphate in one gallon of water.

Once cleaned, a cement floor can be painted with a good deck or epoxy paint.

## Carpeting

If the carpet appears overly worn, consider having it replaced. If hardwood floors are beneath, restore the surface. It is unlikely you will recover the cost of a new carpet in the sale of your home, but it will likely sell faster.

The carpet may only need a thorough cleaning. If this is the case, you can either have it professionally steam cleaned or do the job yourself with rented equipment. Clean badly stained areas with a rug-cleaning product or try equal parts of white vinegar and water.

## CREATING NEW LIVING SPACE

Expanding cramped living space will, providing the improvements aren't too extravagant, add immediate comfort and value to your home. Before going ahead with major structural changes or adding on, consider certain space-saving improvements that require only minor renovation.

Quite often you can enhance the feeling of space just by storing away paraphernalia. Nooks and crannies or even the space under a stairway can be inexpensively converted to a storage area. Overhead shelves can display knickknacks around the perimeter of any room. Narrow bookcases can surround a window or frame a fireplace. Narrow shelves on pantry doors and kitchen cabinets can accommodate extra kitchen supplies. Buyers fall in love with these little niceties, especially in the kitchen, where the chef rules the roost.

Here are some additional space-saving ideas:

- A center work island with built-in drawers and cabinets in the kitchen
- Built-in drawers under platform beds
- Window seats with storage underneath
- Double-rod clothes rack in high-ceilinged closets
- Multipurpose storage modules that double as room dividers

Structural alterations can also make better use of existing space in one of three ways: dividing a large room to make small rooms, combining small rooms to create a larger living area, and converting a room to a multipurpose room. Rooms that are often divided are a large bedroom to create two smaller ones; a living room to form a foyer; and a combined living and dining room to form an eat-in breakfast nook and separate living room. Typical conversions include garage to a family room, screened-in patio to den, carport to more kitchen area or den, and deck to enclosed breakfast room.

Structural alterations can be expensive. Nevertheless, when you're providing more usable space, you'll also be adding value to the house. And converting any structure that already has a floor, a wall, and a roof will be less expensive than building living space from scratch.

Before going ahead with any structural renovation project, do some planning. First, picture in your mind how the improvement will look and how much space it will provide. Next, draft a rough floor plan, keeping in mind door and window locations. Also think about furniture requirements and where you want electrical outlets and light switches. Don't forget to consider how the exterior of the house will be affected. If you're going to, say, convert the carport to a den, try to maintain aesthetic harmony. In other words, be consistent with items like windows and doors, keeping them similar in style, size, and height to the rest of the house.

Another important consideration in the removal of a wall is whether or not it happens to be holding up the house. A load-bearing wall must remain in place, or nearby areas must be reinforced to allow for its removal. But how do you know if a wall is load-bearing? Two rules of thumb apply here. The first is that all exterior walls are load-bearing. The second is that nonload-bearing walls run perpendicular to the floor joists.

When removing walls, you also have to be concerned with what's inside them. The location of wires, heating ducts, and plumbing all have to be considered. Careful planning is imperative in order to save money on the alteration and to assure proper function of the new space.

## Creating a Room in the Attic

Converting the attic to usable living space can be remarkably economical, but attic renovation deserves careful planning. The following are special considerations.

Is the attic floor strong enough? Local building codes will specify the minimum size of floor joists required for support. Most houses have 2 × 6 joists, which may be adequate to support your new attic living space. However, if the span between joists is abnormally large (more than 16 inches), or if your house was built with 2 × 4 joists, then the floor has to be reinforced to provide adequate support.

Does the attic have adequate headroom? Eight feet of headroom is adequate for adults, and less may be adequate if the room is to be used by small children. Headroom can be increased by building a dormer, or you could raise the entire roof, which, unfortunately, is cost-prohibitive. Ventilation could be provided either with vents or with windows that open.

It's also likely that more insulation will be needed in the attic room due to the proximity of the roof to the outside elements. Extra floor insulation shouldn't be necessary as long as the attic room will be heated and cooled like the rest of the house.

To heat and cool the attic room, you could tie in to the existing system. But in most cases it's cheaper to install a baseboard heater and an individual wall-mounted air conditioner, provided that adequate electricity is available.

You also have to consider access to the attic room. Ultimately, the practicality of the room itself depends upon how easy it is to get there. Ideally, you need a stairway that is at least 2 feet 10 inches wide and that rises at no greater than a 35-degree angle. (Stairs any steeper become dangerous.) A ladder or pull-down stairs could be used if you lack adequate space, but they're inconvenient. Here you must think about the function of the attic room. Is the room for kids, or will the in-laws be staying in it and consequently climbing difficult ladders?

## Basement Renovation

Creating more usable space below ground level can be a wise move, provided that the space is properly utilized. A workshop, laundry room, or playroom for the kids is a good idea that provides utility to what otherwise would be wasted space. On the other hand, a den, bar, or library wouldn't be practical or desirable. The reason is that most contemporary home buyers prefer living space above ground, not an inclimate cave below ground.

Renovating a basement involves solving the problem of dampness, ventilation, and lighting. Dampness originates from moisture in the ground that penetrates the walls and floors. It also forms condensation that collects on the basement ceiling. Moisture-repellent paint and a dehumidifier will help reduce some of the dampness, but you should correct the problem before starting to alter the basement.

Ventilation and lighting problems can be solved simultaneously with opening windows. They let in air and light, providing illumination and preventing mold and mildew. Artificial lighting, such as recessed ceiling lights that reflect off the walls, make the room appear spacious and less like an underground cellar.

When you're considering finishing off the basement walls, floors, and ceiling, try to use water-repellent products. Paneling on the walls is preferable to wallboard because it's more resistant to water stains. Wallpaper or paint will peel in the presence of continued dampness. On the floors use moisture-repellent carpet or tile. On the ceiling, acoustical tile is recommended. (More information can be found in a pamphlet by the National Association of Homebuilders titled "Basement Water Leakage Causes, Prevention, and Protection," Washington, DC 1978.)

## Adding on Space

To create an economically sound and useful addition to your house, it's imperative that you plan and evaluate, then plan some more. An addition to your house means the expenditure of a huge amount of money, not to mention a costly long-term mortgage to finance such a project. And it means you, and subsequent buyers, will have to live with such an addition for a long time.

Start by determining the function of the addition and who will be using it. If you intend to make the addition a family room, consider its primary use. If, for example, teenagers are going to watch television or play loud music in it, then you'll want good sound insulation and as much distance as possible from the heart of the house. On the other hand, if toddlers use it for a playroom, you'll want it centrally located for easy access.

Once you determine the function of the room, plan the location of doors, windows, lighting, electrical switches and outlets, as well as the room's location in relation to the rest of the house. You also have to plan storage space and the minimum amount of space required for the optimal function of heating, cooling, ventilation, and electrical supply.

Carefully consider design continuity of the addition as it relates to the rest of the house. In other words, it's better to extend the style and character of the house to the addition than to add on something that looks out of place. This consideration includes such components of style as pitch of the roof and its finish, color of siding, type and location of doors and windows, and wall and floor finishes.

You also have to inquire about local building code requirements. Minimum code specifications are enacted to protect the public, and they may not necessarily agree with what you like and where you'd like it built. It's better to have the job done according to code than to take the chance of ignoring local codes and later having to do the job over again.

Finally, you have to consider such factors as position of the sun and location of neighboring houses in relation to placement of your proposed addition. You don't want to obstruct morning sun from the kitchen or interfere with your privacy.

## IMPROVEMENTS THAT DON'T PAY

Ultimately, there are two essential motivations for making home improvements: to have more convenience and enjoy the added comfort it produces, and to earn a greater return on that prime asset, your home. These two motivations, however, don't always complement each other. You may have $15,000 invested in a room addition, and you may feel that the convenience and comfort derived from it are well worth the investment. However, when it comes time to sell, the buyer isn't necessarily going to pay what you have invested or what you think the improvement is worth.

Home improvements that fail to increase the value of the house typically result from one or more of the following mistakes: overimproving for the neighborhood; poor quality of materials and workmanship; eccentric decor or a style of improvements out of harmony with the rest of the house; and availability of a new house of equal size and location for less money than you are asking for yours.

In most cases adding space is more expensive than planning your space from the bottom up, starting from scratch, as for a new home. Yet, as the price of the new construction soars, so does the cost of the existing housing—and, therefore, the greater your chances of realizing added value, especially when you make appropriate improvements.

### Overimprovement

Homeowners too often overimprove. They make inappropriate improvements that might be suitable for them but are not suitable for the overall marketplace.

As mentioned earlier, buyers will pay for an added bathroom, family room, patio, or certain kitchen improvements, but they won't pay for features like tennis courts, sauna baths, or gazebos. Generally speaking, improvements that give a greater return on invested dollars are those that increase space and function.

This is especially true in the kitchen. Extravagant items, such as trash compactors or top-of-the-line refrigerator/freezers with door spigots and ice makers, will pay back only a small portion of invested capital. Instead, consider installing a center work island with storage cabinets or a microwave oven. Avoid fancy appliances that require a lot of energy and maintenance. Contemporary house hunters have become wary of these. Moreover, keep convenience and ease of living in mind. People crave it. Today, more than ever before, people work hard just to make the mortgage payments; in return they seek as much comfort and convenience as possible during their leisure hours.

Overimprovement is linked to two important rules of real estate appraisal: the *principles of regression and of progression*. The principle of regression says that, where a property of superior quality is placed among properties of lesser quality, the worth of the higher-quality property is diminished; it will seek the value level of the lesser properties. In other words, if you build a $100,000 home in a $50,000 neighborhood, the more expensive home will tend to decline in value toward the $50,000 level.

The principle of progression states the opposite: the worth of a property of inferior quality placed among higher-quality properties will tend to increase, moving toward the value of the surrounding properties. Thus, if you construct a $50,000 home in a $100,000 neighborhood, the value of the lesser-valued home will increase.

Therefore, before you consider any improvement, take a close look at other houses in your neighborhood. Ask yourself whether you will be overimproving compared to standards throughout the neighborhood. If, for example, all the houses within your tract have two bedrooms and one bath, and you're planning to add on a bath and third bedroom, you're overimproving relative to standards within your vicinity. You probably couldn't raise the price of the house much—surely not enough to recoup what you'll pay for the addition.

If, on the other hand, the other homes in the neighborhood have three bedrooms and two baths, then you could begin your addition confident that when you sell you'll receive cost plus return on the space you've added.

You also have to be careful about making improvements in neighborhoods that show signs of decline. You wouldn't want to make costly improvements in the midst of deterioration and devaluation. Many neighborhoods, especially within the inner hub of major cities, tend to decline in value. This can be caused from the adverse affects of crime, poor demand for houses in that area, or the encroachment of commercial land usage. The potential of profiting from your improvement should be measured against location, marketing trends, and buyer demand.

## Eccentric Decor

Nothing keeps a house unsold longer than the choice of flamboyant color schemes. And when you do sell, you'll receive a lot less. Buyers are not going to part with their hard-earned money when your house is decorated garishly.

People want simplicity. To get the most for your home, your best bet is to paint the outside with mild earth tones, such as light tan, beige, or white—not deep shades of red, green, or blue. The same goes with the interior. Avoid metallic wallpapers in dots and bright patterns, red carpets, oddball lighting patterns, and ceiling mirrors. These eccentricities express individualism and do not reflect the conventional tastes of the overall marketplace. Rarely will you find a buyer who shares your individual enthusiasm and will reimburse your investment.

## Overdone Landscaping

An elaborate ceremonial Buddha complete with an expensive oriental garden is great for show, but how many buyers will pay for such landscaping? People want an easy-to-maintain lawn and a few simple shrubs and shade trees, not a botanical jungle that requires huge amounts of labor and expense to maintain.

Keep it simple. Few people will pay for an exotic pond or vine-covered gazebo. Buyers prefer a few fruit trees, some choice shade trees, and a nice lawn.

## Underground Living Space

A basement rec room or family room was once thought of as a sound addition to the house. This is no longer true. Today human beings prefer comfortable living space above grade level. Nonetheless, wasted basement space can be converted to functional space such as a workshop, laundry area, or an organized storage area—areas that today's home buyers will find very appealing.

## Garage Conversion

Converting a garage to a rental unit or family room may seem at first to be a good idea, but financially it's a loser. That's because, believe it or not, most buyers prefer a garage to any kind of livable space. Let's face it, a garage is very practical for storing cars, using as a workshop, and storing whatever stuff can't be put elsewhere. Garageless houses are in low demand among today's home buyers.

## Miscellaneous Luxuries That Don't Pay

An elaborate fenced-in tennis court complete with quartz lighting in Palm Springs carries more buyer appeal than a tennis court in Michigan, but neither has a chance of recouping its investment. The same holds true for swimming pools, shuffleboard courts, opulent statues, and stucco tree houses. These are luxurious items that certain individuals can't do without, but it's highly unlikely the next buyer will find them interesting or be willing to pay for them.

## SMALL IMPROVEMENTS THAT PAY

More often than not, it's the small changes that pay the biggest dividends, especially if they're well-chosen changes. Many of these changes are insubstantial in terms of the labor and materials required, yet they do a great deal to create illusions: illusions of roominess, more headroom, more light; illusions that produce a greater feeling of warmth, security, and serenity.

## Stylish Moldings

A really small improvement that not only adds definable style to a plain house but also gives traditional charm to the most nondescript rooms is the installation of stylish moldings. Dating back to the seventeenth century, when New England colonists used it to give their homes distinction, molding today can be purchased in various shapes and sizes at home improvement centers or lumberyards. It is surprisingly inexpensive and comes in a variety of finishes from prefinished synthetics to unfinished hardwoods.

Moldings will enhance any room when used to frame archways, decorate around a fireplace, flank doorways and windows, or to create framed panels on paneling or bare walls. It can also be used as chair railing in an old-fashioned kitchen or dining room.

About ten years ago, I remodeled an old rustic ranch house in Las Vegas. In the dining room, I applied a light print wallpaper on the walls three feet up from the floor. To conceal the seam at the three-foot level, I surrounded the room with a chair-rail molding. Then, at about eye level on opposite walls, I constructed two rectangular frames made of molding stained the same color as the chair rail. These frames enclosed a swatch of the same wallpaper that was applied below the chair rail. It was a nice touch and dressed up what otherwise would be a drab-looking dining room.

Unfinished moldings can be stained or painted to complement the look of surrounding surfaces. Moldings are then applied with glue or nailed to the walls. (For more information on moldings, see the *Reader's Digest Complete Do-It-Yourself Manual,* Reader's Digest Association, Inc., Pleasantville, NY 1978.)

## The Illusion-Creating Mirror

Mirrors can do wonders in creating the illusion of

more space and light. The objective is to locate the mirror for the greatest optical advantage. The most effective way to do so is to locate the mirror on walls that are perpendicular to exterior window walls. Then the light and view are both reflected from outside, giving the mirrored wall an entirely new dimension of depth. This effect is ideal for small rooms (bathrooms, bedrooms, dens) that have a closed-in look.

Another special application of mirrors is very appropriate for a tiny powder room. If you cover two opposite walls with mirror, the small space will become attractively magnified. Twelve-inch squares of mirror are much easier to apply and less expensive than solid slabs.

Don't forget that mirrored closet doors in bedrooms are among the favorite features sought by today's home buyers. Adding full-length mirrors to sliding doors creates an impressive dimension to any room, especially in the master bedroom, where they create a feeling of luxury and convenience.

## Entryway Enhancement

The objective of enhancing the entryway, foyer, or front hall is to impress or captivate potential buyers when they enter the house. First impressions are lasting ones. Sometimes, with just a little effort, you can enhance the foyer in a way that eventually pays big dividends. (Remember that oak paneling I used in the foyer of that Las Vegas house—how it made such a vivid first impression on potential buyers?)

You can do a number of things to enhance the entryway. Sometimes you can simply apply a well-chosen wallpaper, a framed painting, or a stylish framed mirror. You could even relocate that expensive-looking hand-woven rug from a less conspicuous part of the house and let it impress the guests in the foyer.

Entryway lighting also is important. It should be warm and inviting, not overly bright, especially if you show the house at night.

## Porcelain Restoration

Stained or chipped porcelain bathtubs, sinks, and appliances reflect, in varying degrees, lack of proper care and maintenance. Nevertheless, as the house gets older, it's only natural that wear and tear will inevitably take their toll.

Porcelain is a hard, shiny material (usually white) that lines bathtubs, sinks, and many appliances. If the porcelain surfaces in your house are flawed, they can easily be repaired with porcelain repair paste, available at home improvement centers or hardware stores.

Bad stains or chipped porcelain surfaces downgrade the overall impression made by your house. Such defects will most assuredly be noticed and will be reflected in the buyer's offer price, if there is an offer. Examine the porcelain surfaces throughout your house, and take care of any defects. Beautiful, flawless, and stainfree surfaces will most definitely command a premium when it comes time to sell the house.

## A Graceful Tree

It's surprising what one healthy, beautifully green tree will do to enhance the house and intrigue buyers. One fantastic tree—be it a ficus (fig) or palm, or another derivative of an attractive easy-care tree, strategically positioned in the living room or kitchen—will do wonders for creating elegant ambience in your home. If you give it adequate food, water, and light, it will be yours to enjoy for years to come.

Outside the home, trees can do wonders at enhancing the limits of your property, but appropriate selection is important. Planting small to medium-sized trees at the corners of the property gives the illusion of extending the width of a narrow house. Because they won't outgrow a small or single-story house, Japanese maple and gray birch are recommended for this landscape portrayal.

To accent tall houses or provide contrast to square houses, full-shaped trees are recommended. An excellent choice here is the red maple or honey locust.

To create a privacy screen between properties, plant trees that are low-branched with heavy foliage, such as beech and sweet gum. These trees are also ideal for defining property lines or blocking wind.

Trees that act to screen unsightly views should be low-branched with light-colored foliage to emit a feeling of spaciousness. Cedar and Canadian hemlock are recommended when hedgerows are used as natural screens.

## BIG IMPROVEMENTS THAT PAY

When you're thinking of making improvements to the house, especially elaborate ones, ask yourself the following important questions: Does the improvement add space, function, and convenience? Will it look good or be in harmony with the rest of the house? Are you maintaining a strong house theme or style throughout the house? Will the improvements be in tune with what buyers in your area are looking for? And are you overimproving compared to the rest of the neighborhood?

With the exception of the last question, the answers

to all these questions should be yes. If so, then the chances are very good that you'll make proportionately more, or at least recoup your cost on the improvement when you sell.

The following list identifies big improvements that are likely to show a proportionate return on investment over a five-year period. Bear in mind that this list is not entirely scientific, and external forces like inflation and consumer preference can change over time. These ideas do, however, reflect the educated judgment and opinions of myself, Realtors, builders, and national surveys of today's buyer preferences.

| Improvement | Comment |
| --- | --- |
| Energy-efficient fireplace | Most desired feature nationwide |
| Separate master bedroom/bathroom suite | Buyers love it |
| Walk-in closets | Luxurious and convenient, especially with mirrored doors |
| Center work island in kitchen | Much desired, especially with plenty of drawers and cabinets |
| Butcher-block counters | Attractive and simple |
| Full eat-in kitchen | A must, if space permits |
| Modern kitchen | A must, but not too extravagant; aim to spend less than 5 percent of home value |

| | |
|---|---|
| Second bathroom | Good return if cost is kept to a minimum |
| Finished laundry area | Great feature, especially for the homemaker |
| Vinyl tile kitchen floor | Very popular if maintenance-free |
| Finished hardwood floors | Durable; everyone loves them |
| Bifold doors | Great look and saves space |
| Heat pump | Energy-efficient, especially in areas where an air conditioner is also needed |
| Wood decks or flagstone or brick patio | Appealing and worth the investment |

## FINANCING IMPROVEMENTS

At one time, institutional lenders made home improvement loans, and before funding them, the borrower had to show where the money was going to be spent to improve the property. Today home improvement loans are really second mortgages (also referred to as take-out seconds or home equity loans).

Most of today's institutional lenders don't really care how the borrowed money will be spent. The lender's concern is simply that there's sufficient equity in the property and that the borrower has good credit and is capable of repaying the loan. Besides, the mortgage itself is security against the debt. If the borrower defaults on a second mortgage, the lender can protect its loan interest through the act of foreclosure.

First, it's important to know how much you can borrow against the equity in your home. Most lenders will lend up to 80 percent of the home's current market value, less any existing loans.

## ADVANTAGES OF TAKING OUT A LOAN

Borrowing against the equity in your home is advantageous for a number of reasons. First, when obtaining a long-term fixed-rate loan during these inflationary times, you're able to pay back the long-term obligation with cheaper dollars than those you borrowed. In other words, as inflation continues to erode the purchasing power of the dollar, over time the debt is paid back with dollars that are worth substantially less.

To illustrate this, if you had taken out a loan against your home in 1967 over a 30-year term, you would still be making payments on it today. However, today's loan payments would be made with dollars worth only 31 cents compared to the dollars you borrowed 23 years ago. (Based on the Consumer Price Index, $1 in 1967 was worth 31 cents in 1990.)

Granted, you would have paid interest on the borrowed money ever since 1967. Nevertheless, the rate of interest would have been at a fixed rate of 6 percent, which is much less than what you pay to borrow money today. Additionally, this interest cost is reduced because it's tax-deductible.

Another advantage of borrowing is that inflation raises the future cost of improvements you make today. You pay for your improvements with cheaper dollars when you extend payments for them into the future. Meanwhile, your improvements are appreciating in value because they would have cost you more later.

Tax deductibility is another reason for financing your improvements. Tax reform that was enacted in 1986 created a loophole that is associated with second mortgages. You can deduct interest charges on second mortgage loans up to $100,000. However, the deduction for consumer interest is being phased out (10 percent deductibility in 1990, zero thereafter). Because of these changes in the tax law, it would be beneficial to take out a second mortgage loan to pay off existing consumer debt, which is not tax-deductible, with new second mortgage debt, which is tax-deductible.

You could take maximum advantage of this tax situation by using a portion of your second mortgage loan for improvements, and paying off credit card debt with the remainder of the loan. This way you're paying off more expensive and non-tax-deductible (after 1991) consumer debt and replacing it with cheaper second mortgage debt that *is* tax-deductible.

Keep in mind that it would be unwise to consider a tax break alone as reason enough to borrow. Also keep in mind that new tax rates save no more than 15 cents on the dollar for some people, up to a maximum of 28 cents on the dollar.

## GUIDELINES FOR BORROWING

If you intend to take full advantage of inflation and the tax code to maximize your gains when borrowing, then consider the following guidelines.

### The Longer the Term, the Better

As previously mentioned, with inflation eroding the

purchasing power of the dollar, you're better off extending your loan payments as far into the future as possible. The future cost of your improvements will continue to rise as you pay for them with cheaper dollars.

## Select Only Fixed-Rate Debt

Fixed-rate debt during inflationary times is beneficial to the borrower. Due to the effects of inflation, not only do you pay back the debt with cheaper dollars, but you benefit as the encumbered property and the improvements continue to appreciate. That's why you should select only fixed-rate debt.

On the other hand, adjustable-rate loans favor the lender and are unfavorable to the borrower. Adjustable-rate mortgages (ARMs) came into existence during the hyperinflationary times of the early 1980s. Long-term lenders originated ARMs in order to protect themselves from radical changes in market interest rates. Under terms of the ARM, the rate of interest charged the borrower is adjusted up or down depending on the index rate it is tied to. During inflationary times when interest rates are usually rising, the lender is protected because the borrower must pay more in higher interest charges. This means that ARMs shift the beneficial effects of inflation from the borrower to the lender. ARMs represent a substantial risk to the borrower because of the unpredictability of future interest rates.

However, there are two exceptions to this rule. The first is that within the first four years of the loan, the ARM tends to be cheaper than a fixed-rate loan. Studies have shown that, because the borrower can originate an ARM at a lower rate than that of a fixed-rate loan, it takes about four years for the adjustable-rate loan to match the costs of the fixed-rate loan. Thus, if you intend to hold the encumbered property four years or less, the ARM is favorable.

The second exception is the convertible ARM. This hybrid offers the borrower the option of converting the ARM to a fixed-rate mortgage during a specified time. Under these terms, the borrower can avoid some of the risk of the ARM by switching to a fixed-rate loan when conditions are favorable.

## Avoid Balloon Payments, Prepayment Penalties, and Acceleration Clauses

A *balloon payment* is a lump sum due at the end of a loan obligation: essentially it's a promise to pay an additional amount of cash at some future time. Balloon payments are usually required for loans in which the borrower pays only interest during the term of the loan. If the lump sum isn't paid, the lender usually is legally entitled to begin foreclosure proceedings. Long-term loans that are fully amortized (the principal amount is paid off along with the interest) are much safer because no balloon payment is owed at the end of the term.

If you must obligate yourself to a balloon payment, extend the term as far in the future as possible. This makes the balloon easier to live with because you'll have more time to prepare for its payoff.

A *prepayment penalty* is a clause in a loan agreement which entitles the lender to charge the borrower a penalty for paying off the loan before the end of the term. Six months' interest on the unpaid balance is a common penalty. This penalty covers the lender's cost in reclaiming, and then reloaning, the money you paid back prematurely.

An *acceleration clause*, also referred to as a due-on-sale clause, authorizes the lender to accelerate (make due and payable) the loan balance upon the occurrence of a certain event, generally the sale of the property. That is, if you sell your property, the lender can call the total principal balance due and payable within 30 days. The clause may, as an alternative, give the lender the right to charge the buyer assumption fees and an increased rate of interest.

These items strictly benefit the lender, not the borrower. Any one of these entanglements can inhibit the profitability of your investment. For example, if you allow a balloon payment while arranging a second mortgage, this secondary financing is less attractive to a future buyer of your property, because such a lump sum is difficult to pay off. This means the buyer might be unwilling to pay for your property by assuming (taking responsibility for) the second mortgage, so selling your property may be more difficult.

Also, if your loan contains an acceleration clause, the loan is not legally assumable. Instead, when you sell your property, you must pay off your loan immediately. This seriously inhibits the sale of the property, because now the buyer is required to originate new financing in order to purchase it.

## SHOPPING FOR A LOAN

When you've narrowed down exactly what you're looking for, as well as what to avoid, you're ready to start thinking about where to look for a second mortgage loan. If you're already a customer of a savings and loan association, start there. However, do not accept the first loan offered. Make a few calls to other S&Ls, and compare all the costs. In addition, make a few calls to mortgage bankers and real estate brokers, who may have insight into who is offering the best deals. Just a savings of half a percent in interest can save you thousands of dollars over the life of a long-term loan.

If you're a qualified veteran, a Veterans Administration (VA) loan could be your best bet. Interest charges are usually below the rates for conventional sources, but be prepared for additional red tape and time required to process the loan. The same goes for Federal Housing Administration (FHA) loans. Any person who is employed and has good credit can apply for an FHA loan.

When you're inquiring about mortgage loans, compare more than just interest rates. Check on the annual percentage rate (APR) which reveals the actual cost of the loan. Also ask about the other charges you will have to pay when you take out the loan. These include points (one point equals 1 percent of the loan amount), loan origination fee, application fee, title insurance, appraisal and credit report cost, and, if applicable, the conversion fee on a convertible loan.

Also, beware of rate fluctuations. How long will the rate you're applying for be locked in? Most lenders will charge one point to lock in their quoted rate.

## SPEEDING LOAN APPROVAL

To say the least, applying for a mortgage loan is a huge bureaucratic paper shuffle, especially under the government-sponsored programs of the VA and FHA. The most efficient way to reduce the tedium and speed up the process is to be prepared. You can assist in the procedures by carefully collecting all the pertinent data, then making sure your loan officer gets it quickly.

Before you start, if you have any doubts about your credit, get a copy of your credit report from a local agency. TRW is a national credit-reporting bureau that will supply you with what you need for a small fee. The report will alert you to any surprises or discrepancies listed on the report. Any negative information that appears on your credit report will, of course, require an explanation. Most credit-reporting agencies will try to update a faulty report if you contact them directly.

Also, assemble the financial information you'll need. Having the following information will help speed up the process:

- Bring your checkbook if you're applying for a conventional loan. Some lenders will charge you up front about $300 to begin the process. This fee will cover the cost of the appraisal and credit report.
- You will have to sign employment verification forms, which will be sent to your employer. You can speed up the process by finding out who at your company is responsible for verification. Inform that person that the inquiry is coming, and have it sent to him or her. If you're self-employed, you'll need copies of federal income tax returns for the past two years.
- You'll need the account numbers for all your bank accounts, credit cards, outstanding loans, and previously paid-off loans. Also, you'll need the addresses and branch names of the financial institutions.

By being prepared and supplying your loan officer with what is needed, you can actually speed up the usually slow loan approval process.

# CHAPTER 3

# Cashing In the Equity: Converting Home Value into Income

When you retire, overall living expenses will likely be one-third less than your preretirement costs (see Chapter 1). If your expected income from investments, Social Security, pensions, and other sources still falls short of your requirements, then a smart move is to tap the equity in your prime asset, the house. You have several options available, depending on whether you prefer to remain in your home or move.

## EQUITY-CONVERSION METHODS— REMAINING IN THE HOME

If you decide to stay in the house, four conversion methods are available for tapping income from the value in your home:

- A reverse-annuity mortgage
- A second mortgage loan or refinancing

- A sale-leaseback
- Renting out an accessory room

## Reverse-Annuity Mortgage (RAM)

Many potential retirees have a sizable amount of equity in their homes just waiting to be converted into income. The easiest way to use this equity would be to take out a second mortgage loan; however, most retirees living on fixed incomes cannot qualify for such a loan. For them, a reverse-annuity mortgage (RAM) that pays tax-free income to the borrower—and allows the borrower to retain title and ownership of the home—could be more appropriate.

The increasingly popular RAM is different from other types of loans. As the term *reverse* suggests, the RAM is just the opposite in function of a typical mortgage. Instead of obtaining a lump sum and then making payments to the bank, you get a steady stream of monthly payments (annuity) from the lender, which allows you to remain in your home and maintain your current lifestyle. Each payment you receive increases the amount owed on the RAM. But that loan does not have to be paid off until you die, sell the house, or move. The exception is a *term* RAM, which has a specified maturity. Provisions on reverse mortgages vary from one lender to another, but generally you can borrow up to 80 percent of your equity value in the home. The amount of the monthly payments is determined by a number of variables, including the homeowner's age, the value of the home, the amount, if any, of future appreciation the owner is willing to share, interest rates, and historical appreciation of real estate in the area.

What happens if you or your spouse live to a ripe old age after taking out a RAM? Will you lose your home and be tossed out? No. As long as the mortgage is not a term RAM and is *nonrecourse*, which means you can never owe more than the value of the home and the lender cannot seek repayment from your other assets, you can stay in the house as long as either of you are still alive. The RAM will come due and have to be paid off only when the house is sold, either by you or your estate. From the proceeds the lending institution then gets back the principal paid to you plus costs, which vary from lender to lender and include closing costs, origination fees, interest, and insurance fees for loan guarantees.

Before taking out a reverse mortgage, consider the following:

- Certain types of reverse mortgages allow the lender to receive a percentage of the appreciation of the home. By all means, avoid these. You're better off taking out a reverse mortgage that only requires a charge for interest and closing costs and not a portion of your future appreciation.
- If you sell or move within five years after taking out the reverse mortgage, the penalty for early withdrawal will be prohibitive.
- When determining the amount of equity to give up, most homeowners decide to retain some value as a cushion to borrow against and to bequeath to their children.

For more information on both federal and private reverse-mortgage programs, write to either the American Association of Retired Persons (AARP) Home Equity Information Center, 1909 K Street N.W., Washington, DC 20049 or HUD, Single Family Development Division, Room 9272, 451 7th St., S.W., Washington DC 20410.

## Refinancing or a Second Mortgage Loan

Refinancing your home with a new mortgage is the obvious choice when you own it free and clear of any loans. You can usually borrow up to 80 percent of the home's value. But if you have an existing underlying loan on the property, then you can either refinance or take out a second mortgage loan.

When you take out a second mortgage loan to make use of the equity in the home, you leave intact the existing first mortgage. Most older first mortgage loans are at interest rates far below the current prevailing rate of new mortgages, so if you pay off these older, lower-rate mortgages by refinancing them, you would be eliminating their value by replacing them with a costlier, high-interest loan. But you can earn substantial savings by refinancing if the prevailing mortgage loan rate is *two points or more* below the fixed rate that you're already paying on the first mortgage. The savings you earn each month have to be compared to the costs of refinancing over a reasonable period.

As a rule, refinancing costs about 3.5 percent of your loan amount. This cost represents loan origination fees, credit report, title search, and appraisal. Once you've determined your refinancing cost, divide that by the amount you'll save each month in lower payments. The result is the number of months it will take to break even.

For example, let's say you have a $100,000 loan at 12 percent and want to refinance it with a 9.5 percent mortgage, and the cost of refinancing is $3,500. At 12 percent, your monthly principal and interest payments are $1,029. At 9.5 percent, the payments are $841—a monthly savings of $188. When you divide the $3,500 refinancing cost by the savings of $188, the result is 19, which means it will take 19 months to recoup the cost of refinancing.

Unfortunately, if you're refinancing from an adjustable-rate mortgage to a fixed-rate loan, you won't know when, if ever, you'll break even. Adjustable-rate mortgages are predictable only in the first or second year; then the rates vary according to market index rates they are tied to.

If your first mortgage has a favorable fixed interest rate (9.5 percent or less), you may be better off to maintain the value of the existing low-interest loan by taking out a second mortgage. Assume, for example, that you bought a home 15 years ago for $40,000 with a 30-year first mortgage at 8 percent. The payment for principal and interest is $294 a month, and the remaining loan balance after 15 years of ownership is about $30,000. Since the current market value of the house is $100,000, you therefore have about $70,000 equity in the home.

If you refinance the house at an 11 percent rate of interest, the lender would advance 80 percent of the market value, of which $30,000 must be applied toward paying off the existing first mortgage loan. Consequently, there would be $50,000 in net proceeds ($100,000 × 80% = $80,000; $80,000 − $30,000 = $50,000). The new first loan would require monthly payments of $762 to amortize principal and interest over a 30-year term.

On the other hand, if you arranged a take-out second mortgage for a net amount equal to refinancing ($50,000), at today's rates the lender would charge you about 13.5 percent. For a term of 15 years, the monthly payment would be $649. The total monthly payments on the first and second loans for the next 15 years would be $943 ($294 + $649). After 15 years both the first and second mortgages would be paid in full.

## COMPARING REFINANCING TO A TAKE-OUT SECOND MORTGAGE

| REFINANCING | | | |
|---|---|---|---|
| Amount of Net Proceeds | Payment on First Loan | Term of Loan | Total Amount Paid |
| $50,000 | $762 | 30 yrs. | $274,320 |

| SECOND MORTGAGE | | | | | |
|---|---|---|---|---|---|
| Amount of Net Proceeds | Payment on First Loan | Term Remaining on First Loan | Payment on Second Loan | Term Remaining on Second Loan | Total Amount Paid |
| $50,000 | $294 | 15 yrs. | $649 | 15 yrs. | $169,740 |

In this case, taking out a second mortgage instead of refinancing resulted in a savings of $104,580. Note that the property was refinanced at three points higher than the rate of the older, existing loan. Also note that $30,000 went to pay off the original amount owing. The primary reason that refinancing costs much more than taking out a second loan is the increase in rates of interest. Another reason for the difference is the much shorter term of the second mortgage. The result is a substantial savings in interest paid over the term of the second mortgage loan.

# Sale-Leaseback

Retirees can also stay in their house with a sale-leaseback arrangement. As the term *sale-leaseback* suggests, you sell your home to an investor and then lease it back from the investor. Under such an arrangement, the seller/lessee usually receives at least a 10 percent down payment and a 20- or 30-year mortgage for the balance owing. The investor pays the cost or property taxes, insurance, and maintenance.

On a $120,000 house, for example, a sale-leaseback arrangement with a 10 percent down payment and a 20-year mortgage at 10.5 percent could generate $12,936 in gross income to the seller. The seller would pay about $10,800 in rent during the first year, leaving a net income of $2,136. Add to that $960 earnings by investing the down payment in 8 percent CDs, and the total annual earnings would be $3,096.

The sale-leaseback can benefit both the investor and the seller/lessee. The investor has tax advantages from the ownership interest in rental property. These advantages take the form of deductions for depreciation, mortgage interest, and certain other costs. The seller/lessee receives a down payment and an interest-bearing note, and he or she is no longer responsible for major house repairs, property taxes, and hazard insurance. See Chapter 4 for suggestions about selling your house.

# Rent Out an Accessory Room

Consider making use of empty den or bedroom by renting it out to a tenant. You could earn $300 or more monthly in rental income depending on the quality, size, and the amenities of the rental offered.

Remember that your privacy depends on whether

the rental unit has a separate bathroom and kitchen. If such facilities are not available, the boarder will have to make use of common-area facilities.

And don't forget that if you do rent a room, your house is considered to be income property. This means you'll be obligated to report the rent as income to the IRS. However, it also means you can deduct a proportionate allowance for depreciation. In other words, if 20 percent of the house is rented, then you can deduct 20 percent of the cost of the house each year as a depreciation allowance. See Chapter 6 for more information on depreciation.

## EQUITY-CONVERSION METHODS— MOVING OUT OF THE HOME

Many retirees want to move away from their primary asset. The house is probably too big now for their present needs, especially with the children grown and living on their own. The house they have lived in for so many years has finally become obsolete—but only as it functions for them, not in potential usefulness for others.

Perhaps you have heard the term *trading up*. This commonly used term refers to the act of trading in an old car for a new one or to sell an older, smaller house in order to buy a bigger one when the family grows. In general, trading up is what most of us do when we can afford to move up to bigger and more expensive things.

Upon retirement, unless you're very rich, it's necessary to be frugal with your money, so you might find yourself wanting to do the opposite—*trading down*. Trading down is the act of trading the big, expensive house for a smaller home in order to allow you a certain amount of financial freedom. Because you trade for a smaller, less-expensive one, the result is a substantial savings in living costs. You save on property taxes, insurance premiums, mortgage payments, and maintenance costs. (Think about the drudgery of constantly mowing lawns, cleaning empty rooms, or shoveling snow.) But more importantly, the trade down also offers you more income (in some cases, tax-free income).

The following are the possible alternatives if you intend to move out of your house (trade down) and replace it with another:

- Sell it for all cash
- Sell it on installment
- Rent it with a buy option
- Rent it

Other possibilities considered here involve the replacement home. Is it better to buy or rent? If you buy, is it better to finance or to pay cash? What about paradise on the road in an RV?

Most retirees will probably find that selling the big, expensive home and then renting a smaller home is the best way to preserve retirement money. Nevertheless, everyone's situation is different. Therefore it's better to look at each alternative before making such an important decision.

## Sell for All Cash

When you're totally cashed out of the primary residence, you not only have to consider the tax consequences on the gain incurred on the sale; you also have to think about where to invest the proceeds. If you or your spouse are 55 or older, you can avoid paying tax on up to $125,000 in gain on the sale of your home. If you buy another residence, you also have the option of deferring tax on the gain. (For suggestions about how to sell your home, be sure to read Chapter 4, and for more information on taxes on the sale of your home, please see Chapter 6.)

Proceeds from the sale could be invested in municipal securities or CDs, where you could expect a yield of about 8 percent in today's market. If you don't need all of that cash for retirement but only the income earned if you invest the cash, then you'd do a lot better than 8 percent by considering the other alternatives of selling on installment or renting the house.

## Sell on Installment

If you don't need a large sum of cash immediately, then an installment sale could be the best alternative. This way you could sell the house by accepting a safe, but not exorbitant, down payment and carry back a loan for the going mortgage rate (10 to 11 percent today) on the balance owing. This pretax return is much greater than yields from investing in municipal securities or CDs, which makes selling on installment so attractive.

Bear in mind that selling the home on installment is feasible only if the following two conditions exist.

● You don't need the cash and prefer income from the sale.
● All existing underlying loans on the property are assumable. (Without assumable loans, the buyer is required to pay all cash or to originate a new loan to purchase your home.)

Incidentally, under an installment sale the house is security for the note. This means that if the borrower defaults on your note, you have the legal right to foreclose on the property in order to protect your loan.

Foreclosure, however, is neither cost nor trouble-free, which makes selling on installment a riskier option than selling for cash. Much of the risk can be reduced by requiring a reasonable down payment (at least 15 percent) and by being sure your buyer has good credit.

## Rent with a Buy Option

Renting with an option to buy, like selling on installment, is only feasible when the underlying loans are assumable. That's because when the option is exercised, the tenant will be assuming the existing financing without having to create a new loan.

A buy option (sometimes referred to as a lease with option to buy) is a rental agreement in which the tenant pays extra for an option to purchase the property. The buy-option agreement spells out the price and terms at which the tenant may buy the property. Under a typical buy-option contract, the owner of a property gives the tenant the option to purchase the rented property at a specified price, within a set period of time, and for an option fee. You could, depending on the size and quality of your rental, earn an extra $300 or more in monthly income by offering your tenants an option to buy it. You continue to pay necessary property taxes and insurance on your property until the option is exercised.

The tenant pays the option fee in installments with the rent. These payments are applied toward the established purchase price or the down payment. As an example, let's say you can rent the house for $900 monthly. But, even better, you could offer the tenants a buy option and charge an extra $300 a month in option fees. The additional $300 is applied to the purchase price or the down payment.

The buy option has a number of advantages over simply renting the property.

- This added feature usually can mean a quicker sale of your property. More potential buyers will be attracted to your property because they can make the down payment on installment via the monthly option fees instead of the large up-front pool of cash usually required.
- Because they expect to own it eventually, buy-option tenants tend to make improvements to the property, and for the same reason they will usually take better care of the property than renters.
- You, the homeowner, get to keep the option fees already paid if the tenant fails to exercise the buy option.
- When the option is exercised, you don't have to pay a sales commission to a real estate agent. On a $120,000 sale, that's typically a savings of $7,200 when the commission is 6 percent.
- The tenant also benefits under this creative strategy because he or she avoids costly loan-origination fees by assuming the existing financing.
- If handled properly, a buy option is safe and secure. A neutral trust, such as a title company, should handle the transaction when the option is exercised. This way both the tenant/buyer and seller are protected, ensuring that all liabilities are being paid. The tenant/buyer makes one payment into the trust, the trust disperses all funds to pay the liabilities (loans, taxes, and insurance), and the seller receives what's left over.

## Renting

Renting your property would probably be the least

advantageous way to dispose of it. You wouldn't receive nearly as much income from the property as you would under the other three alternatives. However, renting it could be advantageous for tax purposes or if you expect the house to appreciate substantially in the future.

## ONE COUPLE'S COMPARISON OF THE ALTERNATIVES

Every situation is different, so be sure to look at all the alternatives. A logical way of doing so is to state the costs and benefits in tabular form. The remaining tables in this chapter illustrate the options available to a retiring couple who owns a mortgage-free house worth $120,000:

## DISPOSITION OF $120,000 MORTGAGE-FREE HOUSE

| Alternative Used | Proceeds from Sale | Proceeds: Interest from 8% CDs After 1 Year | Property Taxes and Insurance | Mortgage or Rental Income from House | Total Annual Earnings |
|---|---|---|---|---|---|
| **Cash Sale** | $111,600 | $8,928 | 0 | 0 | $8,928 |
| **Installment Sale** | $18,000 | $1,440 | 0 | $12,220 | $13,660 |
| **Rent with Buy Option** | 0 | 0 | $1,800* | $14,400 | $12,600* |
| **Rent** | 0 | 0 | $1,800 | $10,800 | $9,000 |

The preceding table illustrates under the cash-sale alternatives that the couple receives $111,600 ($120,000 less 7 percent selling costs) net proceeds. This amount is then invested in 8 percent CDs.

Under the installment-sale alternative, the couple receives a 15 percent down payment ($18,000) and a $102,000 mortgage at 10.5 percent for 20 years payable at $12,220 annually. In addition, they invest the down payment in 8 percent CDs.

Under the rent-with-buy-option alternative, the couple receives $1,200 monthly ($14,400 annually) in rent, of which $300 monthly applies toward the purchase price. After the option is exercised, the tenant/buyer will pay property taxes and insurance.

Under the rent alternative, the couple simply rents the property for $900 a month ($10,800 annually).

Lastly, if the couple decides to remain in the house, they have (besides a second mortgage or refinancing) three alternatives in the disposition of it.

The table below illustrates three alternatives the couple has if deciding to remain in the house. Under

## DISPOSITION OF $120,000 MORTGAGE-FREE HOUSE WHILE REMAINING IN THE HOUSE

| Alternative Used | Total Annual Earnings |
| --- | --- |
| Reverse Mortgage | $4,766 |
| Sale-Leaseback less $900/month rent | $3,096 |
| Rent an Accessory Room at $400/month | $4,800 |

the reverse-mortgage alternative, they take out a reverse annuity mortgage that pays them $397 monthly ($4,766 annually.)

Under the sale-leaseback alternative, the retirees sell the house on installment, then lease it back from the investor. The sellers accept a $12,000 down payment and carry back a mortgage at 10.5 percent for 20 years payable at $1,078 monthly ($12,936 annually). They rent the house from the investor at $900 monthly, for an annual cost of $10,800. Therefore, because they pay out $178 less then they take in, their net annual earnings are $2,136. Add to that the 8 percent annual CD earnings ($960) on the $12,000 down payment and the result is total annual earnings of $3,096.

In the rent-an-accessory-room alternative, the couple simply rents a vacant room to a tenant for $400 a month.

## Analyze the Alternatives

Based on the examples given, the couple will receive the greatest return by selling on installment when they move out of the house. If they decide to remain in the house, the greatest return results from the reverse-mortgage alternative. Whether you choose to stay in your house or move out, be sure to analyze both the costs and benefits of your alternatives. Your decision will depend on your particular situation, of course, but you should now be able to make a well-informed decision.

## BUYING VERSUS RENTING THE REPLACEMENT HOME

Once the primary residence is either sold or rented, you must decide whether to buy or rent a replacement home. Before making your decision, consider the following possibilities.

- Buying offers you the tax benefits of deducting mortgage interest and property taxes as well as the possibility of price appreciation. (See the "Great Places to Retire To" section in Chapter 7 for more suggestions when buying a condo.)
- Renting allows you more mobility and is a cheaper way to establish a residence (no down payment or closing costs); also, you won't have to worry about problems that may come up when you sell the property.

## Buying: Should You Pay All Cash or Finance the Replacement Home?

If you can afford it, should you pay cash for the replacement home or finance it? Retirees definitely should *not* pay all cash. Once they tie up a large portion of their money in a home, it's often very difficult to get it back. They're better off in a more liquid position, in which funds are available for emergencies or short-term investment opportunities.

The best time to borrow money is when you're in good health and working with an adequate income, not when you absolutely need the money and are not working. Even if you can afford to pay all cash for the replacement home, you're better off making a minimum down payment and taking the maximum home loan available.

## Why Renting Is Sometimes Better

With few exceptions, in most cases you're better off renting a replacement home at first instead of buying

one right away. That's because most people will be
unfamiliar with property values in the community
they move to. You may have stayed in the area occasionally while on vacation, but unless you've lived
there for a while, it's difficult to make a careful eval-
uation of the overall marketplace.

Also, if you decide to travel extensively after retirement, renting will allow you more mobility. If you're
on a month-to-month lease, you won't have to pay rent
or worry about an unattended home. Simply put the
furniture in storage and take off.

# CHAPTER 4

# Selling Your Property

Sooner or later, you may find it necessary to liquidate certain realty holdings. Whether or not you use the services of a Realtor or sell the house yourself and save the commission, keep in mind that, on average, it takes about three months to sell a home. Obviously then, selling the house is by no means an easy chore. This is especially true if you expect to get your asking price.

## GENERAL GUIDELINES TO SELLING

• If you're in a housing market where properties are in high demand (a seller's market), try to sell the property yourself to avoid paying a Realtor a commission. On the other hand, if you're in an area where there are few buyers (a buyer's market) and many properties, you should hire a Realtor so you can sell your home as quickly and successfully as possible.

● Time the sale of your property to coincide with highest level of market activity. It is always better to sell during the spring and fall seasons—that's when most buyers are looking for property (especially if they have children attending school). Avoid trying to sell the property during winter, particularly between Thanksgiving and New Year's Day. During these holiday times, home buyers are usually too preoccupied to take the time necessary to purchase a home.

● Price the property right. To arrive at the right place, you can pay $150 or more for an appraisal, or you can study the local market and determine the value yourself. For a quick off-the-cuff evaluation, concentrate on the value per square foot of the comparable properties in your neighborhood. You must first establish the lowest offer you'll accept. Then adjust your price upward from this point. Most buyers like to negotiate, so allow yourself a little flexibility. Price the property reasonably above the lowest you'll accept in order to stimulate bona fide offers.

● If you decide to carry a second mortgage or deed of trust when selling the property, be sure to include a "due-on-sale clause" in the document. This clause states that all your remaining equity in the note will be due and payable if the property is ever sold to a person other than the one you are selling to. It will protect you if the property is subsequently sold again before you are paid for it. If you decide later that you'd prefer to receive monthly payments after all, you have the option to ignore the clause. But never limit your flexibility by excluding the clause from your note.

● Always use deeds of trust (if available in your

state) rather than mortgages as the instrument to secure the debt. Mortgages are more cumbersome and take much longer to foreclose on.

• Always use a neutral third party escrow agent, usually a title company, to handle all the necessary documents (mortgages and deeds). If the buyer defaults, the escrow agent can return to you all the documents relevant to your property.

• If the buyer is to assume your existing loans and is paying your down payment in cash, be sure he or she follows through. Never transfer the title until you are sure the buyer has actually made the down payment and assumed any loans.

• You need to put your property, inside and out, in top physical condition. That means thoroughly cleaning not only the living area but also the exterior grounds, basement, and the garage. If necessary, paint it inside and out. Give special attention to the entryway—it is the first thing prospective buyers will see. You also need to fix all those little things you've tolerated for so long. You know what they are: leaky faucets, cracked receptacle and switch covers, loose doorknobs. These can detract from the beauty of your home and will surely be reflected in the price offered.

• Avoid the cluttered look by putting excessive furniture in storage; then rearrange and organize what's left to make rooms appear larger. Prospective buyers are looking for spaciousness.

## IF YOU DECIDE TO SELL THROUGH A REALTOR, FOLLOW THESE GUIDELINES:

• Find a real estate agency that advertises aggressively and has many agents or belongs to the MLS

(Multiple Listing Service). The more exposure you get, the better.

● Be sure you have confidence in the agency you list with.

● When you do list your home, allow yourself as much flexibility as possible. Never list for extended periods like six months or a year. A three-month listing should be sufficient. If you become dissatisfied with the service you receive from the agency, have the listing agreement rescinded for lack of performance. This can usually be accomplished by contacting your local board of realtors. It isn't necessary to wait out a listing agreement if you feel you're being mistreated.

## IF YOU DECIDE TO SELL THE PROPERTY YOURSELF, FOLLOW THESE GUIDELINES:

● Never advertise your property address. You want to stimulate interested buyers, not lookers. However, you do want to put the price in the ad. This will eliminate many calls from unqualified buyers. The heading "For Sale by Owner" always attracts attention. Most buyers automatically figure they can buy at a bargain price because of the absence of a commission.

● When the prospects begin calling be prepared. You should know the following information: lot size, age of the house, square feet of living area, names of nearest schools, and major cross streets.

● You should also be prepared to answer questions based on your loan documents: Is the loan(s) assumable? If so, what is the interest rate? How much are the property taxes? Is there a prepayment penalty? If so, will the lender waive it if the buyer obtains a mortgage from the same lender? What is the current principal balance owing on the loan? Is there a tax and insurance impound account? If so, what is the balance in that account?

• In addition, you will need copies of the following documents: the paid tax receipt for the previous year, survey of your property, and evidence of title.

• Don't mistate or inflate the facts. You are likely to be tripped up by some unassuming buyer who will refute a false statement instantly. Then the deal is off, for nothing will so undermine the confidence of a buyer as a misstatement knowingly made by one who is attempting to sell real estate.

• It's a good idea to put down in writing the features you want to present when making a sale. These may include such things as the view from your property, proximity to shopping, and quality of construction. Writing down these features will help to anchor them in your mind so they can be recalled at the proper time.

When it's finally time to show your home to prospective buyers, all of your work will definitely be worth the effort; well-prepared sellers receive more *and* better offers.

# CHAPTER 5

# How to Build a Multiproperty Estate

A multiproperty estate is the result of continual investment in additional properties using the earnings and appreciating equities of other properties. The foundation of your estate probably will be the home you already own.

After years of price appreciation and mortgage paydown on the principal residence, it's time to think about investing in a second house. But before you proceed with the estate-building process, ask yourself the following questions:

- Is the house you're moving from in habitable condition? All improvements should be completed (you're not renting a fixer-upper), and the house should be clean and in move-in condition.
- Do you have sufficient capital including the down payment and renovation funds to invest in a second house?
- What will be your plan of operation?

Assuming that the house is rentable and that you have sufficient funds, essentially you have two options: you can stay in the primary residence and rent the second house to tenants, or you can move into the second house and rent out the primary residence.

Personally, I recommend the latter option. Experience has taught me that it is much simpler and less expensive to rent out the house you are in, even with the inconvenience of moving. During a certain four-year period in my career, I purchased a house about every six months. I would move in, spend about half a year renovating it, and then rent it out when I saved enough money to buy another property. This way I had prospects coming to my door instead of meeting them at the other property. And it was efficient because I made renovations while living in the property instead of transporting supplies over to the property to work on it.

About the only meaningful disadvantage to working this way is that you have to move your household belongings every time you acquire a new house. However, the advantages outweigh the inconvenience of moving often. Here's why:

- It's more efficient. That's because it's simpler, less time-consuming, and more cost-effective to renovate the house while living in it. When renovations are completed and you've saved enough money for a second house, then you can rent the principal residence and move to the second house.

  Furthermore, you won't have to continually drive to the second house to make renovations or to show it to rental prospects.
- The house you're living in will show better than the unfurnished and unoccupied second house.

# KEY FACTORS TO THE WEALTH-BUILDING PROCESS

Building a successful multiproperty estate depends on four key factors:

- Price appreciation
- Tax reduction ability
- Refinancing benefit
- Selling at a profit

## Price Appreciation

As a realty investor, you have inflation as well as time on your side. Depending on the strength of the real estate market in your city, you can expect your property to appreciate 6 to 10 percent annually. This is the result of a combination of inflation and mortgage paydown. And as time passes, rents on income property can be increased. This means that the property you purchase today with a small down payment can eventually develop positive cash flow.

## Tax-Reducing Ability

Real estate ownership allows you to retain more spendable income because you pay less in income taxes. Homeowners are allowed deductions for mortgage interest, interest on home-equity loans, and property taxes. Income-property owners have the additional benefits of a depreciation allowance and certain expense-related deduction. By putting together all of these tax shelter benefits, most property owners can show a taxable loss on their tax return when actually they're earning positive cash flows.

## Refinancing Benefit

Refinancing benefits evolve over time as the property continues to appreciate. Once the equity attains a worthwhile value, you can borrow against it to make additional investments.

## Selling at a Profit

Property owners can avoid or defer tax on the earned gains when selling real estate. Theoretically, you could avoid or defer tax until you die.

In summary, creating a multiproperty estate doesn't just happen overnight. You begin with the first property and add to it some sweat equity and time to help increase its value. Before you know it a few years have gone by, and the house has substantially increased in value. By then, you can either use some of your savings or borrow against the equity for a down payment in order to buy a second house.

Consider the following scenario that involves subsequent investments in several houses over the next twenty years. Today, in year one, you buy an undervalued fixer-upper and move into it. You occupy the house for the next three years, making renovations that increase its value. You also start saving for a second property.

Beginning in year four, you buy a second house with accumulated savings. You rent the first house, move into the second house, and begin renovating it.

About three years later, in year seven, you buy house number three. It could be purchased with accumulated savings or by refinancing house number one, since its value has likely doubled in seven years. Then you rent house two, move into house three, and begin renovating again.

During the next thirteen years you continue the process of buying, renovating, and renting properties. At the end of twenty years, depending on your success as an investor and general market conditions, you should be able to generate enough income to comfortably retire on the house!

# CHAPTER 6

# Income Tax Savings from Your Home

Although real estate's ability to shelter income has been slightly reduced by tax reform, owning a home or other improved property remains the preferred tax shelter. This chapter attempts to clarify the complicated tax laws pertaining to real estate and to help you recognize a tax-reduction opportunity.

## DEDUCTIBLE MORTGAGE INTEREST

The IRS allows taxpayers to deduct interest paid on home mortgages up to the original purchase price plus the cost of any improvements. This deduction is limited to interest on $1 million and only applies to your principal residence and a second home. (If you took out your first or second mortgages before October 13, 1987, you can deduct all the mortgage interest, regardless of the total amount.) Repayment of the loan's principal, of course, is not deductible.

Taxpayers also may deduct interest on up to $100,000 for a second mortgage loan (home-equity loan) on their primary residence or vacation home. Again, there is no limit if the loan was originated before October 13, 1987.

## POINTS AND REFINANCING

Lenders of home loans generally charge *points* or *loan fees* to underwrite a mortgage loan. Regardless of what such charges are called, if they are for the use of money they constitute interest and are therefore tax-deductible in the year paid. For the fee to qualify as deductible, the home has to be used as security for the debt, and the purpose of the loan must be to buy, build, or improve the home.

Fees paid to obtain a loan secured by any other type of property (anything that's not a principal residence), or for a purpose other than to buy, build, or improve the residence, must be deducted over the term of the loan, even though the entire loan fee was paid up front when the loan was issued.

*VA loan points* or processing fees are *not* tax-deductible as interest. Such fees, which are paid by the seller, are a selling cost and should be deducted from the home's *adjusted gross selling price*. (See "Calculating Your Capital Gain" later in this chapter.)

*Penalties* and *prepayment* fees incurred when prematurely paying off your mortgage are fully tax-deductible in the year paid.

Deductions for interest paid on refinancing your mortgage are allowed up to the purchase price of your home plus the cost of any improvements you've made. Thus, you cannot deduct interest paid on the portion of a mortgage loan that at the time the debt is incurred exceeds the cost of improvements and the purchase price of the property.

## INTEREST ON IMPROVEMENT LOANS

Interest on a loan to make home improvements is fully deductible in the year paid. However, the cost of making the improvements cannot be deducted but should be added to your home's cost. The cost of home repair and maintenance is *not* tax-deductible for your principal residence, unless it qualifies as home-office expense or as an expense related to renting part of your home.

## DEDUCTION FOR PAYMENT OF PROPERTY TAXES

As a rule, state and local property taxes on your principal residence are deductible in the year they are actually paid to the tax collector. Note that many homeowners make payments to an impound account, such as a bank escrow or title company, for later disbursement. If so, the money is deductible in the year the property taxes are paid from that account to the tax collector.

## DEDUCTIONS FOR HOME-OFFICE OR RENTAL USE

If you use part of your home for an office, or rent part of your home to tenants, you're entitled to deduct expenses related to this business use. (Qualified renters also can deduct part of their rent if a portion of their home is used for business purposes.) A structure unattached to the home and used in connection with the taxpayer's business also will qualify.

To qualify, the business portion of your home must be used *only* for business purposes and on a regular basis. (The room where your spouse watches television while you work does not qualify.)

## DEDUCTIBLE HOME-OFFICE EXPENSES

The home-office expenses that may be deducted are the portion of all ordinary home expenses, plus depreciation, affecting the business area. These expenses include home utilities, hazard insurance, mortgage interest, repairs, and property taxes. The depreciation deduction is based on the proportionate amount of the home's value allocated for the business area.

There are two ways to determine what portion of these amounts to deduct. One is to divide the number of rooms that constitute the business area by the total number of rooms in the house. The other is to find the percentage of the home's total area that constitutes the business area and multiply that figure by the total expenses. So, if you find that your business area comprises 20 percent of your home, for example, 20 percent of your ordinary home expenses affecting the business area are tax-deductible.

### Reporting Rental Income and Deductions

Rental income and expenses are reported on Schedule E of your tax return. You report the gross amount received and then deduct such expenses as mortgage interest, property taxes, maintenance costs, and depreciation. The net profit is added to your other taxable income within the passive-loss limitation.

Security deposits are treated as trust funds and are

not reported as income. However, if your tenant breaches the lease agreement, you are entitled to use the security deposit as rent. At that time, you would report it as income.

## RECORD-KEEPING REQUIREMENTS

As mentioned earlier, deductions for interest paid on loans other than mortgages depend upon how the borrowed money is used. Taxpayers who borrow must trace how they use the loan proceeds from the day they take the loan until the day it is repaid.

This is only one of the requirements that make complete records essential. The following procedures are suggested to simplify record keeping and to avoid losing deductions because of improper record-keeping methods:

- Maintain separate accounts for personal, business, and investment use.
- Be sure the debts incurred for investments can be traced to the investment. A taxpayer who spends the proceeds of a loan within 15 days qualifies for the interest deduction; however, if the loan proceeds sit longer than 15 days, the IRS will base eligibility for the deduction on the first purchase made from the borrowed funds.
- Consider home-equity loans as opposed to other forms of loans. They are tax-deductible and don't require as much record keeping.
- Refrain from writing checks on stock margin accounts for purposes other than buying stock.
- Keep cancelled checks, receipts, and other records related to income tax deductions for at least three years. Also keep receipts concerning home improvements as long as you own the house.

These receipts substantiate expenses that will be used to increase the cost basis in order to reduce taxable gain. (For more on cost basis, see "Calculating Your Capital Gain," later in this chapter.)

## CAPITAL GAINS

When you sell a capital asset such as real estate or stock, the amount by which the price you get exceeds the price you paid is called a *capital gain*. Thus, if you paid $10,000 for an asset and then sell it for $25,000, you have a capital gain of $15,000. Capital gains are currently taxed as ordinary income.

## Tax Savings When You Sell the House

Homeowners may use two perfectly legal techniques to *avoid* or *defer* paying taxes on the gains they earned when selling their home.

## Deferring Tax on the Sale of a Residence

The tax law allows homeowners to defer paying tax on the capital gain when they sell their home. To qualify for this deferral, you must meet the following three tests:

1. *Principal residence test*—You must have used your old house as your principal residence, and you must buy a replacement that you use, or intend to use, as a principal residence for tax-deferral purposes. You may have only one principal residence at a time. You cannot defer tax on the profitable sale of a principal residence by

purchasing a summer cottage; and you cannot defer tax on the sale of a second home.

2. *Time test*—You must buy or build your replacement house and use it as a principal residence within two years of the sale of the old house.

3. *Investment test*—For you to defer taxes on the entire gain, the replacement house must have a value equal to or more than the amount you receive from the sale of the old house. If the replacement house costs less, you must pay tax on the gain that exceeds the value of the replacement house.

If you qualify under these three tests, tax deferral is mandatory. Odd as it may sound, the IRS *requires* you to defer paying taxes if you can do so.

## Deferring Tax in an Exchange

For tax-deferral purposes, exchanging houses or trading is considered the same as a sale. If you make an even exchange or pay additional cash, you pay no tax on the trade. However, if you receive cash in the trade for the replacement house, you generally must pay tax on the amount of cash you receive.

Taxpayers can defer capital gains indefinitely by exchanging one property for another. The exchange must be of like properties—such as two real estate parcels to be held for investment purposes—in order to qualify for tax deferral. You could not, for example, trade your principal residence for a 10-unit rental building or vice versa. Also, the mortgages being assumed must be at least as large as those given, and the equity obtained must be at least as great as the equity given. The difference in equity between the two properties is made up with a note.

|  | Property Given | Property Received |
|---|---|---|
| Selling price | $80,000 | $150,000 |
| Mortgages owing | 50,000 | 100,000 |
| Equity | 30,000 | 50,000 |

A trade-up, which this example illustrates, qualifies for tax deferral on the full capital gain because the mortgages being assumed are larger than those given, the equity is larger than that being given, and no boot or cash was given. (The $20,000 difference in equity between the property given and that received is made up with a note.)

## ONE-TIME TAX-FREE SALE OF RESIDENCE

Not only can you defer taxes, but once in your lifetime, if you are 55 or older when you sell or exchange your principal residence, you can *avoid* tax on profits up to $125,000. To claim this exclusion, you must meet the following requirements:

● You must elect to avoid the tax.
● You must be 55 or older before the date of the sale.
● For at least three out of five years before the sale, you must have owned and occupied the house as your principal residence. (If you became incapacitated and had to enter a nursing home or similar facility, you would only have to occupy the home for one out of five years to qualify for the exclusion.)

You may not use this exclusion if you sell only a partial interest in the home.

If you and your spouse own the home jointly and file a joint return in the year of the sale, only one of you needs to meet the minimum age requirement and qualify under ownership and residency requirements. However, once one spouse has claimed the exclusion, the other spouse may not claim it later.

Approach the tax-free option with caution. Because this is a once-in-a-lifetime exclusion, consider deferring the tax instead if the gain from the sale of your home is substantially less than the $125,000 exclusion and you plan to reinvest the proceeds in a replacement home. You can defer paying tax on your gain by purchasing a replacement house at a cost equal to or more than the sales price of the old house. Then your exclusion is still available for when you sell the replacement house without buying another home.

## CALCULATING YOUR CAPITAL GAIN

To calculate your capital gain, subtract the adjusted cost basis of the property from its adjusted sales price.

The *adjusted cost basis* equals the purchase price plus any non-tax-deductible closing costs incurred at the time of purchase and the cost of any capital improvements made during ownership. Examples of non-tax-deductible closing costs are title fees, escrow charges, and legal fees. Capital improvements (not repairs) include a swimming pool or a new roof. Then subtract from this total any tax deductions claimed during ownership for business use or rental of the house to tenants.

The *adjusted sales price* equals the gross selling price of the house less all selling expenses. These expenses include the sales commission, advertising costs, escrow fees, title fee, and FHA or VA loan points paid by the seller.

## VACATION HOMES

If you own a vacation home, you may get some tax benefits by treating it as a second home and deducting mortgage interest and property taxes.

Remember that mortgage interest is deductible only on the taxpayer's first and second homes and is capped at $1 million. A vacation home can be a condominium, apartment, house trailer, motor home, boat, or house. If a vacation home is rented, taxpayers can claim losses of up to $25,000 if their adjusted gross income is $100,000 or less; this deductible is reduced when adjusted gross income is over $100,000.

Some taxpayers try, by renting out their vacation homes, to reduce their taxable income by deducting business expenses or even taking a loss (expenses in excess of income) associated with renting out the vacation home. The IRS uses the following tests to determine whether you are allowed to deduct expenses or losses:

● If you rent out the vacation home for less than 15 days, expenses associated with the rental (except for interest and property taxes) cannot be deducted. Any profits from the sale of the rental are not taxable, provided you meet the conditions for tax deferral or tax-free sale of a residence.

● If you rent out the vacation home for 15 days or more during the year and meet the residency test, your expenses not beyond gross rental income are fully deductible. (Any income above—operating gain—expenses is taxable.) You meet the residency requirement if your personal use of the home exceeds either 14 days or 10 percent of the number of days the home is rented.

● If you rent out the vacation home for 15 days or more, and your own usage is less than 14-day/10 percent test, you are not considered to have used the home as a residence during the year. In this case, losses as well as expenses may be deductible. The tax courts have allowed loss deductions when the owners made little personal use of the vacation home and proved that they bought the house to earn a profitable amount on resale.

As these tests suggest, the tax law prohibits most homeowners from deducting losses on the rental of vacation homes.

## DEPRECIATION

Depreciation is a percentage reduction that represents the loss of value of an asset over its physical life. Instead of an actual expense to the investor, depreciation is simply a bookkeeping entry.

If you buy property to earn rent, then you must depreciate its cost over several years and deduct a part of it each year (assuming the property has a useful life of more than one year).

Depreciation makes it possible for real estate investors to earn substantial net income from their properties while actually showing taxable losses. Thus, real estate is a type of tax shelter: the taxable loss (actually a net gain, or profit, before depreciation deductions) can shelter other income from taxation.

### What Can Be Depreciated?

Property is depreciable if it meets all three of these conditions:

- It must be used to generate income (e.g. in business or to earn rent or royalty income).

- It must have a measurable useful life of longer than 12 months. A property's useful life is an estimate of how long you can expect to use it in your business or to earn rent or royalty income from it.
- The IRS defines depreciable property as something that "wears out, decays, gets used up, becomes obsolete, or loses value from natural causes."

## Figuring Depreciation

The two basic types of assets, real property and personal property, are depreciable under different rules. In general, real property is limited to straight-line depreciation, or reduction of an equal amount each year. Personal property may be depreciated using accelerated methods of depreciation, which means the taxpayer can deduct a larger share of the property's value in the early years of ownership. By carefully distinguishing between these two types of property, taxpayers can increase their tax benefits in the initial years of ownership.

## Depreciating Buildings

Residential real property is depreciated using the straight-line method over a useful life of 27.5 years. Thus, one year's depreciation deduction on a $100,000 rental home (not including the land value, as land is not depreciable) would be $100,000 ÷ by 27.5, or $3,636. For nonresidential structures such as office buildings and shopping centers, the useful life is set at 31.5 years. In the month you purchase the building or put it in use, you must use one-half month's depreciation deduction.

# PASSIVE INCOME AND LOSSES

A *passive activity* is any activity that involves the conduct of a trade or business in which you do not materially participate. Any rental activity is defined as a passive activity even if you materially participate in it. A trade or business includes any activity involving research or experimentation and, to the extent provided in the regulations, any activity connected with a trade or business or for which the IRS permits a deduction as a business expense. You are considered to participate materially if you are involved in the operation of the activity on a regular, continuous, and substantial basis. Participation by your spouse will be considered in determining whether you materially participate.

For the tax years beginning after 1986, deductions from passive activities may only be used to offset income from passive activities. Any deductions that exceed such passive income result in a "passive-activity loss." This loss may not be deducted against your other income but may be carried over and applied against passive income in future years. In addition, any allowable credits from passive activity may only be used to offset future tax liability allocable to your passive activities.

## Some Passive Losses Can Offset Wage or Business Income

Remember that no matter how much you participate in real estate rental activity, it is still considered a passive business, and you can offset any losses only against income and gains from other passive investments. In other words, real estate losses cannot shelter wages or income from an active business.

However, there is a major exception to this rule. Certain investors can qualify for up to $25,000 in loss allowances. To qualify, the investor must meet an income test and a participation test. If you have an adjusted gross income (AGI) of $100,000 or less, you can deduct the full $25,000 loss allowance. If your income is less than $150,000, only 50 percent of the amount by which your AGI exceeds $100,000 is deductible. An AGI $150,000 or more means you cannot take the $25,000 loss allowance deduction. Thus, if the AGI is $130,000, the allowance is $25,000 − (.50 × $30,000), or $10,000; if the AGI is $150,000, the allowance is zero.

Active participation is the other requirement needed in order to claim this loss allowance. Active participation is defined as (1) ownership of 10 percent or more of the value of the activity during the entire year in which the deduction is claimed; and (2) responsibility for the operation of the business. You must meet both of these conditions. You can hire others to handle details for you—make repairs, for example—but you must be involved in the decision-making process of the business to meet this participation rule.

## Passive Losses Are Carried Forward

Any passive losses investors cannot use during one tax year are carried forward as *suspended losses* and used in one of two ways:

1. Unused losses incurred in prior years and carried forward apply against income or gains from passive activities in future years. They can be used only to shelter income in later years for the same or other passive investments.

2. Unused suspended losses from prior years can be used to reduce any gain investors realize when they dispose of their investment.

# ADMINISTRATIVE REQUIREMENTS

The IRS has imposed certain administrative requirements for investing in tax shelters, reporting rental income, and keeping records.

## Registration of Tax Shelters

The principal organizer of a tax shelter must register it with the IRS no later than the day on which interests in the tax shelter are first offered for sale to investors. If the principal organizer fails to register the tax shelter, another member of the shelter can do so.

Under registration requirements, the seller must provide investors with the tax shelter identification number issued by the IRS. Investors then report this number on their tax returns.

The IRS can assess penalties for failing to meet these requirements.

## Reporting Rental Income and Deductions

Rental income and expenses are reported on Schedule E of your tax return. You report the gross amount received and deduct such expenses as mortgage interest, property taxes, maintenance costs, and depreciation. The net profit is added to your other taxable income. If you realize a loss, you can reduce the amount of your other taxable income within the passive-loss limitation.

If you use the cash-basis (income and expenses are charged to the period when they are received or made and not when they are incurred) accounting method, you report rental income in the year you receive payment.

Security deposits are treated as trust funds and are not reported as income. However, if your tenant breaches the lease agreement, then you are entitled to use the security deposit as rent. At that time, you would report it as income.

# CHAPTER 7

# Retiring Worry-Free: Ideas and Suggestions

Up to this point, we've been primarily concerned with increasing house value and with disposing of the house before retirement. Now let's explore the possibilities of where to go and what to do after retirement, including the disposition of other realty holdings.

## PLANNING

With proper planning, retirement can be the beginning of a new and exciting phase of your life—rather than merely the end of an old one. Attitude is important. Think of retirement as a new chapter in the biography of a lifetime, a chapter in which you do the things you want to do—not chores you have to do.

Like most major endeavors, a satisfying and productive retirement, while relaxing, requires thoughtful planning. Essentially, when you finally decide to retire, it's best to keep the whole procedure uncomplicated.

## TURN OVER REALTY HOLDINGS
## TO A PROPERTY MANAGER

If you intend to relocate out of state, you'll either have to sell all your realty holdings or turn the responsibility of managing them over to a competent manager. Don't even think about trying to manage them yourself if you are living out of state. It's just not practical. You need someone to handle repairs, collect rents, and show vacancies. These tasks are better handled by someone living in the vicinity of your holdings.

Licensed property management companies charge, on average, about 10 percent of the gross rent for their services. This fee, of course, varies depending on the size and character of the property being managed. Management fees for units within a resort area, for example, can be upwards of 20 or 30 percent.

Management responsibilities include collecting rent, paying expenses (but not the mortgages) that arise during normal operation, showing vacancies, and remitting to the owner a report of the manager's activities, along with a monthly check for proceeds, if any.

As in any other business, property managers include their share of incompetents and crooks. The unscrupulous and incompetent managers can cheat owners of deserving income.

Although being an absentee owner makes you a candidate for being ripped off by less-than-legitimate managers, forewarned is forearmed. After all, being aware of how you can be cheated is a form of defense in itself!

Unsuspecting absentee owners can be taken advantage of in several different ways. The following practices are a few that frequently take in naive owners:

• Charging unsuspecting owners for nonexistent expenses

- Renting a vacant unit, collecting the rent, and continuing to declare to the owner that the unit remains vacant
- Overcharging for maintenance and repair

There are, unfortunately, even more involved schemes; some haven't even been dreamed up yet. In most cases, the opportunity for cheating the owner occurs during turnover, when the tenant vacates the rented unit.

When I moved to Florida, I turned management responsibility of four rented properties over to what I thought to be a reputable company. Everything went smoothly until a vacancy occurred in one of the units.

First the property manager reported to me that the place was a mess, that the tenants had absconded with, among other things, the refrigerator, washer, and dryer. (How was I to know whether he was telling the truth? At the time, I was living 2,000 miles away.)

After the manager spent a small fortune of my money getting the place back in habitable condition, it then went vacant for three months. If all this weren't enough, the property manager talked me into selling the troubled property. I reluctantly agreed, and that's when peculiar things began happening.

One day after the property had been up for sale for a month, the manager called and said he had shown the place the day before and that this day we should have an offer to purchase it. Great news, right? Wrong!

It turned out that the prospective buyer for my lovely (or formerly lovely) three-bedroom ranch house on a half-acre of land overlooking Las Vegas claimed that the foundation was faulty. After careful inspection of the house and its foundation, it was the prospective buyer's opinion that the house was worthless in its present condition.

Well, upon hearing this horrible news over the phone from my manager, not only did I get upset, but

I felt entirely helpless as well. After spending a few sleepless nights trying to resolve this dilemma, I made a decision.

For some reason, I smelled a rat in the cheese. That day I called Las Vegas and proceeded to order an independent inspection of the foundation in question. Within three days, I had a complete written report confirming my suspicions—the foundation was A-OK. Furthermore, I would later discover that the manager was a silent partner of the prospective buyer who had claimed the foundation to be faulty. It was their intention to purchase my house for 50 cents on the dollar, then split the profits upon resale.

I guess if there's a moral to this story, it's that you shouldn't trust just anyone, licensed or otherwise. Be sure to get references before hiring someone, especially if he or she will be handling your money.

## PROJECT RETIREMENT INCOME

When projecting income for retirement, the first place to check is with your employer. Find out how much you can expect from your pension plan.

Regarding Social Security benefits, you can check the status of your account by calling the Social Security Administration (SSA). Call the U.S. Department of Health and Human Services, and ask for card number SSA-7004, a request for statement of earnings. You can also obtain the card directly from SSA by writing to SSA, P.O. Box 57, Baltimore, MD 21203.

### Individual Retirement Accounts (IRAs)

In general, the earliest you can begin withdrawing from an individual retirement account without pen-

alty is age 59.5. The latest is April 1 of the year following the year in which you turn 70.5. The minimum
distribution you must take depends on your life expectancy or the joint life expectancy of you and your
beneficiary.

Ordinarily, any withdrawals from your individual
retirement account before age 59.5, except in cases of
death or disability, are hit with a 10 percent tax penalty. But a little-known provision in the tax code
allows you to withdraw your money before 59.5 without penalty. Recently the IRS laid out three acceptable
plans for doing this. These plans are the life-expectancy method, the annuity plan, and the amortization
plan.

The catch is that you must withdraw the IRA
money under a system of equal amounts each year.
These periodic amounts are based on life-expectancy
tables published by the IRS and available at the library. Also, once you begin taking money out early,
the IRS won't let you stop or change your withdrawal
plan for five years or until you reach age 59.5, whichever takes longer.

## Life-Expectancy Method

The easiest plan is the life-expectancy method.
Simply divide your IRA balance by your life expectancy. The result is the amount you can withdraw
each year, subject to income taxes but no penalty.

Find your life expectancy in IRS Publication 590,
"Individual Retirement Arrangements." For a free
copy, call 1-800-424-FORM. The IRS uses identical
life-expectancy tables for men and women.

As an example of this plan, let's say you're 50 years
old and want to begin withdrawing from your IRA,
which has a balance of $250,000. According to the IRS
tables, your statistical life expectancy is 33.1 years.

Divide your $250,000 balance by 33.1, and the result is a first-year withdrawal of $7,553. Next year, you refigure how much you can withdraw by dividing the IRA balance by 32.1.

## Annuity Plan

To gain access to more money in the early years of withdrawal, you can use the annuity plan. It is designed on an annuity formula that's also based on life expectancy but adds an assumed future return on the capital you have invested. Under the annuity method, you get a faster payout, because it allows you to use any reasonable mortality table. Mortality tables generally give shorter lifespans than the IRS life-expectancy tables, so the annual payout is greater.

If you're 50 years old with a $250,000 IRA, with a given annuity factor of 11.109, and based on an assumed return of 8 percent, you would be entitled to a penalty-free distribution of about $24,304 a year ($250,000 × .08, then divided by 11.109).

Be careful when using the annuity plan, especially if you are figuring it yourself. You'd be wise to hire an actuary or CPA to calculate the annuity factor, because the chances of doing it incorrectly are high. If the computation is wrong, the consequences are a 10 percent federal penalty on the amount withdrawn. To make matters worse, some states levy matching penalties.

## Amortization Plan

The third alternative, the amortization plan, works like a mortgage in reverse: it gives you equal payments each year. To make your calculations, take your IRA balance, figure a reasonable yield it should earn (i.e. 8–10 percent—the IRS lets taxpayers decide what yield is reasonable), then calculate how much you have to withdraw annually to bring the balance to zero by the time of your death.

If you're 50 years old, have an IRA balance of $250,000 and a life expectancy of 33.1 more years, and expect an 8 percent yield on your account, your annual payout under this method would be $21,698. You can compute this amount on any calculator that does amortization schedules.

### Additional Considerations

No matter what plan you decide to use to avoid the early-withdrawal penalty, what you take out of your IRA is taxable as ordinary income (assuming you deducted the contribution in the first place). If you made a nondeductible contribution, then you'll only pay tax on the portion of your withdrawal that represents return on your investment.

Before you begin mining your IRA gold, you should make some careful considerations. You may want to spend the money now, but will you have enough left for later years? After all, the point of most IRA saving is to accumulate some rainy-day money specifically for the later years of your life, when you may have less control over your financial circumstances than you did before.

## MAKE A WILL

Proper planning also means getting your estate in order. Be sure your will is up to date—you should consult with your attorney to assure that it is done properly. Failure to draft a will leaves your estate to be determined by your state's intestate statute and government tax collectors. If your estate has to be settled in

court, the surviving family members (heirs) have to
endure delays of up to one year and thousands of
dollars in unnecessary court costs.

Also, if your inheritable assets exceed the $600,000
exemption from state taxes, you should hire a capable
lawyer to set up a trust agreement.

## PLAN FOR HEALTH CARE
## AND INSURANCE NEEDS

Probably the greatest fear of a future retiree is the
thought of losing everything one worked for to the
costs of a prolonged illness. If you're close to retirement, check with your employer to determine whether
you can extend health insurance coverage when you
stop working. Another alternative is Medicare supple-
mental health insurance. For more information on
this coverage check with the American Association of
Retired Persons (AARP).

Regarding life insurance, the older you get, the
more expensive it is. The less expensive term insurance is better if you are in your midfifties or older. Get
enough coverage so that the death benefit, invested at
a conservative rate of return, would generate enough
income to replace current earnings.

## REDUCE RISK

Just before or upon retirement is a good time to
switch your investment strategy from that of an ag-
gressive mode to one of safety. Certificates of deposit
are ideal for retirees. They're secure and liquid and
help replace your salary. Also, if your portfolio is big
enough, consider high-quality tax-free municipal
bonds.

## Certificates of Deposit

If you decide to sell your realty holdings, the best thing to do with the proceeds is to buy one-year certificates of deposit (CDs). Purchase them in chunks of $50,000 or more. Most financial institutions offer their best rate on CDs of $50,000 and above. Invest in your CDs at different institutions, so as not to exceed the $100,000 limit on FDIC insurance.

Now that some of the ailing financial institutions are closing, the healthy ones are under less pressure to compete by offering high rates. This being the case, be shrewd in how long you tie up your money in CDs. You gain little by locking in cash for five years instead of one year.

To find the best CD rates, check the ads in the business section of local newspapers and the *Wall Street Journal*. Be sure your CDs are insured by the federal government. Deposit insurance on deposits up to $100,000 is provided by the Federal Deposit Insurance Corporation (FDIC) through the Savings Association Insurance Fund (SAIF) for savings and loan associations and the Bank Insurance Fund (BIF) for savings banks and commercial banks. If you aren't sure whether your financial institution offers this protection, ask.

Time the purchase of your CDs so that they mature every month or two throughout the year. Then you can simply roll over (reinvest) each CD when it matures, or you can spend the money however else you like.

## High-Quality Bonds: Best Investment for the Nineties

High-quality bonds promise to be a good investment

vehicle during the 1990s. That's primarily because long-term and short-term interest rates are likely to fall (during the early 1990s), driving up prices of bonds issued by the U.S. Treasury, state and local governments, and stable, profitable companies. Thus, the bonds you buy now are likely to be worth more in a few years.

## U.S. Treasury Securities

For safety, liquidity, and price appreciation, there's no better worry-free choice than bonds issued by the United States Treasury. Treasury bonds are liquid, meaning that they are easily converted to cash. You can do this by selling them through a securities' broker or bank. New issues are noncallable, which means the government cannot make you redeem them for cash before maturity.

The greatest feature of Treasuries is they're exempt from state and local taxes. Additionally, Treasuries are virtually risk-free, with almost no chance of default. You will get your money back unless the United States government collapses. And you can buy them commission-free directly from the government. To do so, write to the Bureau of the Public Debt, Department F, Washington, DC 20239, or phone your nearest Federal Reserve bank or branch.

## Municipal Bonds*

---

*This section is contributed by Howard Marcotte, Municipal Bond Specialist for Dougherty Dawkins of Naples, Florida.

Municipal securities (munis) are the debt obligations of states, their political subdivisions, and certain agencies or authorities. The municipal bond market is one of our nation's most remarkable institutions. It provides a mechanism whereby more than 50,000 state and local government units can issue securities to raise money for public purposes, such as water and sewer systems, schools, turnpikes, and hospitals.

A distinguishing feature of munis is that their interest income is exempt from federal income tax. And, in most states, interest received from securities issued by governmental units within the state is also exempt from state and local income taxes.

Upon issuance of a muni, the issuer promises to make periodic (usually every six months) specified interest payments. The interest rate, or coupon rate, cannot be changed during the life of the security (unless, of course, it's a variable-rate security). Since the coupon payment is fixed, the price of existing bonds must be adjusted to reflect changing market conditions. When the price of a bond rises above its nominal (face) value, it is said to be selling at a premium. A bond whose price has fallen below face value is said to be selling at a discount. Premiums are created when market interest rates fall (that is, the interest rate on new issues falls below those on previously issued securities). The price of existing securities rises to make their yield consistent with yields on newly issued securities. The opposite occurs when market interest rates rise; existing security prices fall, and discounts are created.

Municipal securities have an extraordinarily good record in paying interest and principal on time. Virtually all new issues of municipal securities are being originally offered by means of official statements or offering circulars, which describe in detail the financial condition of the issuer or, in the case of bonds, such as industrial revenue bonds, the financial condition of the user or lessee. From these documents, the potential investor can determine the likely risks involved in the investment.

Payment of interest and principal of general obligation bonds is secured by the full faith and credit of the issuer, and is usually supported by the issuer's unlimited taxing power.

Revenue bonds are secured by a pledge of net or gross income derived from tolls, charges, or rents paid by users of the facility built with the proceeds of the bond issue. Public projects financed by revenue bonds may include highways, bridges, airports, and water sewage treatment facilities.

Most municipal bonds are sold in serial form; that is, a portion of the issue comes due periodically, in anywhere from 6 months to 50 years or more. Thus, a large municipal bond issue usually consists of many separate serial maturities, each of which often has its own coupon rate.

Most bonds are issued in denominations of $5,000 or integral multiples of $5,000. Bonds are also available in minimum denominations of $5,000.

Interest on bonds is usually payable semiannually. On notes it is usually paid at maturity.

If you invest in municipals directly, you pay a smaller broker markup if you invest at least $25,000 for five bonds of a single issuer.

The goal of any investor should be to maximize an after-tax rate of return consistent with the amount of risk he or she is willing to accept. For taxpaying investors, tax-exempt munis often provide an ideal investment to accomplish this goal. This is particularly true where the investor's primary objective is to obtain the highest possible after-tax income.

Some of the newer types of bonds—zero-coupon, compound interest, and multiplier securities—are attractive to investors seeking long-term capital accumulation for an education fund, retirement, or other long-range savings goal. Whatever type of muni you decide on, look for investments rated "A" or better.

The municipal department of your securities dealer or commercial bank can answer your questions about a specific municipal issue and help you define your investment objectives. These professionals can provide you with information about current offerings in both the new-issue and secondary trading markets and can assist in selecting the muni most suited to your needs.

## Should You Spend Principal?

When you retire, you may wonder whether it's wise to spend your principal (the savings or investments that are earning interest, as opposed to just the interest earned). The answer is no: don't spend your principal unless it is absolutely necessary.

Instead, leave the principal intact while earning interest on it. Of course, if you knew precisely when you were going to die and you didn't have a spouse or family to care for, you could arrange a timetable to spend the principal so that you would arrive at a zero balance upon death. But realistically we have to face the fact that we're not going to live forever. And unfortunately, with the exception of suicide, we don't know the exact day we're going to die.

If it's absolutely necessary, however, you could spend a portion of principal. For example, you might need to do this for some cash to tide you over until Social Security benefits or your company pension kicks in.

## PAY DOWN MORTGAGES

You can save thousands of dollars over the life of a mortgage by prepaying it. The savings might surprise you. You'll especially benefit on income property by earning more cash flow after the loans are paid off.

For example, assume you have a $75,000, 30-year fixed-rate mortgage at 10 percent. Add $100 per month to the $658 payment, and you'll pay it off in 17.5 years and save $78,000 in interest charges.

The sooner you start prepaying a mortgage, the more you'll save. That's because of the structure of a typical amortized mortgage. During the early years, the majority of your payment is applied to interest, while a small portion is applied to principal. In the preceding example, of the first $658 payment, $625 is applied to interest and $33 to principal. Even after 12 years, the payment is split $549 for interest and $109 for principal.

Prepaying the mortgage can be as simple as attaching a note to the lender that the extra amount is "applied to principal." Think about it: Trading off 17.5 years of prepaying the mortgage at $100 monthly will save $78,000 in interest charges. That amounts to prepaying $21,000 over 17.5 years to earn $78,000 in savings.

Secondary financing on income property also can be prepaid. Take, for example, a property with an existing second mortgage. When you bought the property, you arranged the second mortgage with the seller for $30,000 at 10 percent interest amortized over 10 years at $397 per month. Currently the property is rented, and because you are paying on the second mortgage, you receive no positive cash flow. (The income from the rented property equals the expense.) You could prepay the second mortgage by $100 per month, thereby paying off the second mortgage in about half the term.

With careful planning, you could time the early payoff of a second loan to coincide with your retirement date. This would not only save you thousands in interest, you would also earn more monthly income at a time when you could really use it.

## GREAT PLACES TO RETIRE

Have you ever thought about why you live where you live? Most people haven't. Allow me to tell you a short story relevant to this sometimes bewildering question.

I was born in Detroit, and with intermittent treks to Europe, Florida, and California, I spent the better part of 28 years being educated and working in Michigan. After graduation from college, I moved to Los Angeles and later got married. Eventually we had a little girl, and when she was old enough I would tell her stories about the cold winters in Michigan.

I'd tell her how, as children, when snow and sleet would turn to slush, making the streets an ice-covered playground, we'd hop a ride behind passing cars; how we made extra money shoveling snow off the neighbors' sidewalks, how we had to scrape frozen ice off the windshield before driving the car; and how, when it was extremely cold, it was necessary to breathe through the nose instead of the mouth or else your breath would freeze in your mouth.

I went on to tell her about snow skiing in northern Michigan. One day it was so bitterly cold—14 degrees below zero with a wind chill factor of minus 40—that the big toe on my left foot became frostbitten. Ever since that memorable day, whenever I'm exposed to cold weather, my frostbitten toe aches.

When I finished that story, she responded, "Daddy, why did you live in such a cold place so long?" I said that I didn't realize how much I enjoyed warmer climates until I experienced them, which unfortunately didn't occur until the age of 24.

That was a long time ago. Today many people believe life elsewhere is too good to be true. Yet they stay where they are and make alibis about why they can't move. They tolerate unhealthy environments, putting up with gridlocked freeways, bad air, and over-crowded and crime-infested cities. If you're 40 years old, you have the better half of an adult lifetime ahead of you. Why would you want to spend it on a cold, snow-covered, smoggy, and overcrowded freeway?

During your working years, your home becomes the focal point of a labor lifestyle. You spend most of your time there, usually in preparation to go back to work. When you retire, your home is merely a temporary layover. The kids are no longer there, except for occasional visits. You travel more. You're more active outside. Home is simply a pleasant part-time place to rest.

Of course, it would be great to retire and afford a big house in Palm Springs or a luxurious penthouse along Wilshire Boulevard. But most of us have to trade down the mansion in order to retire. Fortunately a lot of good alternatives are available.

## Vacation Home: Preretirement Style

A vacation home can save you money by providing your lodgings while you're on vacation. After retirement, you'll have plenty of time to travel. During the working years, spend your vacations in the second home, and save vacation dollars doing it. It's a place to relax, to enjoy fixing up, and to dream about someday living there full-time.

But before selecting this alternative, consider what kind of climate you like, how far you want to move from family and friends, shopping, restaurants, what you need for health care, and what cultural or sporting activities suit you. While vacationing in different places, talk with people who live and work there. Also, compare the costs. Find out how much it costs to rent or buy a home. What about state and local income taxes, property taxes, and sales tax? All these levies vary substantially from state to state, and they can take a big chunk from a fixed income.

By having a vacation home, you'll also benefit psychologically from knowing you have a home when you retire. You ease the transition to retired life. Arranging the vacation/retirement home now saves you the stress related to the move later on.

Furthermore, although investing in a vacation home and renting it when you're not there usually won't produce positive cash flow, it does produce tax deductions (see Chapter 6) and is likely to appreciate in value.

## Paradise on the Road

Have you ever thought about taking your home with you, living on the road in a recreational vehicle? Imagine what it's like living out of an RV. You could visit the kids, friends, or whomever and discover interesting places on the way. Think of it . . . no rent or mortgage payments.

Of course, it helps if you like to drive long distances. You'll also be more inclined to enjoy this type of lifestyle if you're a camping or exploring enthusiast. You might want to try it part-time, traveling in the RV six months; then staying at home for the rest of the year. This way you'd have the best of both worlds.

Realistically, the best way to find out is to rent an RV for a month and try it on for size. Go a few places, and see if you like the lifestyle.

## Paradise, Las Vegas Style

Imagine, if you will, living in a high-desert valley surrounded by picturesque mountains and breathing mostly warm, dry air. Of course, there's lots more to do than just breathe in Las Vegas, because it's the entertainment capital of the world.

No longer the so-called "sin city" of the Southwest Territory, Las Vegas is a mushrooming metropolis boasting over half a million residents. In fact, it's growth- and retirement-oriented. Currently under development is a massive retirement community of 250,000 acres called Summerlin.

Unlike higher-priced housing markets, Las Vegas is a remarkably inexpensive place to live. Rents, housing prices, taxes, and food costs are all below average. Citizens of Nevada also benefit from the absence of state and local income taxes.

With the exception of summer, the high-desert climate is appealing to most people, as it's moderate in temperature and very dry. During the summer, although the humidity averages only 10 percent, the temperature frequently exceeds 100 degrees.

Regarding sports, you have the hometown perennial favorites, the UNLV Runnin' Rebels basketball team considered by some to be the only game in town. The town also boasts the Las Vegas Stars, which is the San Diego Padres' AAA minor-league baseball team.

By 1995, high-speed bullet trains will whisk passengers from Vegas to Disneyland, in Anaheim, California—a distance of 300 miles—in about an hour.

The spectacular Las Vegas Strip is a wonder in itself. So bright is the maze of neon that the lights literally illuminate the night for miles around.

Of course, if you're going to relocate to Las Vegas, you should be familiar with the local gaming terminology. Here are a few relevant terms of interest:

Juice     The person who recommends someone for a casino job.

George    A person who tips, or tokes, the dealers. A "super George" is a generous tipper.

Stiff     A nontipper. Someone who wins money while gambling and for whatever reason doesn't leave a gratuity.

Counter   A person who, while playing the game of blackjack, "counts" the tens in the deck of cards to gain an unfair advantage.

If you like to dine at low-cost gourmet buffets, then Las Vegas is the right place for you. Resorts such as Caesars and the Golden Nugget serve wonderful four-star buffets. On the lighter side, the local townfolk prefer Binion's Horseshoe as a great place for casual dining and gambling.

To entertain the kids and the young at heart, Circus Circus is renowned for live circus shows as well as a great amusement arcade.

Unlike crowded places like Atlantic City, Las Vegas doesn't charge you for parking, nor do you wait in line to spend your money. Although the town is rapidly growing, there's still plenty of available land for future growth.

Nearby attractions include Lake Mead, a reservoir formed by the construction of the Hoover Dam, itself located 30 miles to the south. You can even ski Mt. Charleston, just a 40-minute drive from downtown. Then you have San Diego and Los Angeles, both a five-hour drive to the southwest.

Of course, not unlike any other vision of paradise, this glittering city in the desert does have certain negative attributes. It goes without saying that you must control your gambling, as compulsive wagering is a sickness that can ruin what otherwise would be a healthy bankroll. That's the major detriment. Another

is the summer heat. With the exception of desert landscape, trees and natural flora are scarce. And the city,
for the most part, lacks certain cultural amenities,
such as theaters and museums.

For those who can overlook these deficiencies, Las
Vegas is a friendly town with plenty of activities that
will interest almost anyone, especially retirees.

## Paradise, Gulf Coast of Florida Style

Most undiscovered paradises eventually are discovered
and inevitably become overcrowded with transplanted
northerners. Miami and Fort Lauderdale, which are
densely populated cities along the Atlantic Seaboard,
are prime examples of this unfortunate phenomenon.
The opening of interstate highways is the primary
reason for the growth of the Atlantic Seaboard cities.
And these areas have been popular and accessible ever
since the early 1900s.

However, the southern gulf coast of Florida was
almost inaccessible until the 1940s. It was then that
the Tamiami Trail (Tampa to Miami) was completed,
making what I call paradise accessible from both the
Atlantic Seaboard and the northern states.

Today in southwest Florida, waterfront properties
command a premium price, especially beachfront
properties on the gulf. Typically, any gulf-front home,
be it a condo or a single-family residence, appreciates
in value, on average, 20 percent annually. Similar
homes that are located inland (not facing the gulf)
appreciate at a much lower rate of 6 to 8 percent.

This remarkable rate of appreciation for waterfront
properties is primarily the result of two key economic
forces: strong buyer demand and the limited supply of
waterfront property. Strong buyer demand arises from
the influx of retirees relocating from the north. They

move away from the cold weather and the hustle and bustle of the Northeastern Corridor or the suburbs of Chicago, desiring nothing more than a beachfront home in the sunshine. They have sold their big, expensive home for three times what they paid for it, and now have plenty of cash to spend on a replacement home. The supply of waterfront property is limited because there just isn't any more land left to build on. Therefore its price continues to spiral upward much faster than that of inland property, which is still plentiful.

## Condos Can Be Better than Houses . . . Sometimes

If you intend to retire to Florida, or for that matter anywhere else in America, there are a few important things you should know about condominiums (systems of ownership in multiunit structures where each living unit is individually owned but the unit owners jointly own the common areas and land). First, if you have never purchased or rented a condo before, you should consider it when retiring. A case in point is my condo unit with its many amenities —the boat slips, pool, restaurant, and tennis courts. If I had to rent or purchase a single-family residence that offered these amenities, it would be much more expensive than a comparable condo. (Probably in the neighborhood of $500,000 or $1 million to purchase, and perhaps $5,000 monthly to rent.) To make matters worse, I would have the added expense of maintaining the lawn and building. In contrast, my condominium unit cost only $110,000 to purchase. On an annual lease, it rents for $800 monthly (with seasonal rentals during the winter going for about $2,500 monthly). The homeowners' association, of which all condo owners are automatically a part, allows members to vote on major decisions affecting the complex and charges dues to cover maintenance and operation of common areas. My association dues are only $105 monthly, and they include trash removal, part of the hazard insurance, and lawn and building maintenance. (Lawn maintenance alone on a single-family home would cost $80 monthly.)

Essentially, the reason condo living is much less expensive than living in a comparable single-family home is that all the costs are shared among the owners of the condominium association. The costs of the pool, tennis courts, boat slips, and the like are shared among 400 owners, instead of borne by one.

Being a part owner and having access to so many great amenities is the best reason for living in a condo. But there's more. Although you pay a monthly association fee, it definitely has its benefits. You don't have to be concerned with lawn or building maintenance because someone else does it for you.

However, condominiums—especially when they're located in Florida—frequently make poor investments, usually because there's an oversupply of them. Generally speaking, condos that are valued in the midrange, say $75,000 to $100,000, are the least desirable as an investment. On the other hand, condos valued in the low or high price range tend to be good investments, especially if they're waterfront property. This variance reflects the supply: there happens to be an oversupply of midpriced condos and a shortage of cheaper and higher-priced units on the market nationwide.

Before you go ahead with the purchase of a condo, you should check into several important concerns:

● *Soundproofing*—Keep in mind that condo living is similar to apartment living. In most cases, that means you'll have neighbors living above or below your unit and sharing common walls with you. Inadequate soundproofing between adjacent units is, by far, the number one complaint among condo dwellers. Before purchasing a condo, check with other owners within the association to determine whether they have problems with noise levels from adjoining units. Better yet, have the neighbors in all the adjacent units turn on their stereos and TVs at normal level. Then, while inside the unit you're thinking of purchasing, listen for sound from the adjoining condos.

● *Association provisions*—Condominium associations have certain rules, typically referred to as covenants, conditions, and restrictions (CC&Rs), which may contain unreasonable limitations that may affect you. Before purchasing any condominium, you should get a copy of the CC&Rs and read them carefully. Watch out for specific restrictions, such as limitations on rentals, pets, number of vehicles, and children.

● *Association's financial condition*—Be sure to check the financial condition of the condo association before making an offer to purchase a unit. Beware of an insolvent association, because later on you may be levied with a special assessment to make the association solvent.

Take the time to talk with two or three current owners of the association you plan to buy into. Ask them what they like or dislike about the project and whether they would buy there again. The information you receive may help you decide whether to buy.

## CONVERT EMPTY NEST TO INCOME

Instead of retiring *on* the house, some people may decide to retire *in* the house. In that case, it may be advisable to earn some extra money.

One way is to rent out the empty space in your home. You might even think about starting a home business. What about all those plans you had for a home business when you didn't have the time? Now is the time to capitalize on your knowledge, skills, and interests.

These approaches may ease the unpleasant feelings some people experience when they become "empty-nesters." If you don't already know what empty-nesters are, then you probably haven't experienced the phenomenon. Essentially these are people whose children have moved out of the house and into homes of their own, creating an "empty nest."

You may have experienced similar feelings when your children moved out of the house. Instead of wallowing around the house missing them, consider turning the situation to your advantage. You may find that your empty nest is actually overflowing with golden eggs of opportunity.

## SEMIRETIREMENT

A man regarded as synonymous with hard work and creativity, Thomas Alva Edison, semiretired for health reasons to a winter home in Florida. There, where his health was gradually restored, he lived another 40 productive years (next door, by the way, to Henry "I've got a better idea" Ford). During his waning years, Edison was asked when he planned to retire. He stood silent for a moment, then shouted his reply: "The day before the funeral!"

Although most people admired Edison's obsession with time and labor (he slept only four hours per day), it's not for everyone. But if work is your pleasure, then semiretirement can be a work-style paradise for you. That's because you're doing work you want to do, not work you have to do.

Whatever you choose, best of wishes to you and yours on a new and what I hope will be rewarding stage of your life.

# CHAPTER 8

# Commonly Asked Questions About Retirement, Income Taxes, and Real Estate

The following questions and answers address important topical issues regarding retirement and income taxes in relation to real estate.

## MOTOR-HOME DEDUCTIONS

**I'm considering borrowing to purchase a recreational motor home. Can I claim it as a second home (vacation home) and deduct 100 percent of the interest from my taxes?**

Yes, you can if you don't own another vacation home and the vehicle has a kitchen, bathroom, and bedroom—and as long as the loan is secured by the motor home. The deduction is also good for houseboats or anything the IRS will consider as a second home. Your principal residence and one other residence such as a vacation home qualify for the deduction. However, keep abreast of the current tax

131

laws. There has been some talk that the IRS is going to exclude recreational vehicles and boats from the definition of second homes, even though they meet current requirements.

## 401(K) WITHDRAWALS

**If I'm retired, can I withdraw money from a 401(K) plan at age 55 without paying penalties?**

Yes, you can withdraw money from a 401(K) plan after reaching age 55 without paying the 10 percent penalty. You will, however, owe income tax on the money withdrawn. Other circumstances allow you to take out money before age 59.5, without penalty: when you're disabled, when a distribution is made under a court-ordered divorce decree, or when you receive the money in equal periodic payments over your life or the life of you and your beneficiary.

## DEDUCTIBLE INTEREST

**When is mortgage interest deductible?**

Interest on loans to buy your principal residence and a second home is 100 percent deductible. The deductibility of mortgage interest doesn't become questionable unless you refinance your home or take out a second mortgage.

## LIMITS ON INTEREST DEDUCTIONS

**What are the limitations on the deduction of mortgage interest?**

Mortgage debt incurred on or after October 14, 1987, is divided into two kinds of indebtedness, each with a separate limit. The first is "acquisition indebtedness," or debt used to acquire or substantially improve a residence. Interest on such loans may be deducted for loans up to $1 million for up to two residences. The other type of debt is "home equity indebtedness," which is any debt other than acquisition indebtedness secured by one or two residences. The deduction for interest on such loans is limited to loans for up to the fair market value of the residence plus improvements, not to exceed $100,000.

All mortgage interest incurred on or before October 13, 1987, regardless of amount or purpose, may be deducted. It is treated as acquisition debt and is not subject to the $1 million limit.

# INTEREST DEDUCTION FOR RAW LAND?

**Can I deduct interest on a loan for land that I plan to build a house on?**
Interest on unimproved land is considered personal interest, which is being phased out as a deduction. Personal interest is 20 percent deductible for the year 1989, 10 percent for 1990, and not at all thereafter. Once you begin construction, 100 percent of mortgage interest is deductible.

# POINTS

**Are the points charged by a lender deductible?**
Yes, they are. Points on a loan to buy your house can be 100 percent deductible in the year the loan is issued. However, the points cannot be borrowed as part of the loan amount; they must be paid separately. If the points are added to the loan proceeds, then they must be amortized over the life of the loan.

Points on a second mortgage or refinancing must be amortized over the term of the loan. When the house is sold, the remaining points are deductible. There is an exception: points on VA or FHA loans are not deductible.

## CLOSING COSTS

**I purchased my first house in 1987. The following closing costs were charged: points, appraisal, inspection, title report, and credit report. Which of these costs can I deduct from my federal income taxes?**

If points are paid out of your private funds (not included in the loan proceeds), they are deductible in full the year they are paid. If the points are added to the loan proceeds, then the points are amortized over the life of the loan. The other closing costs are not deductible. However, the nondeductible closing costs can be added to the cost basis of your house. This will reduce the taxable gain, if any, incurred when you sell.

A special note about points and refinancing: when you refinance your home, points are always deducted over the life of the mortgage, regardless of how they are paid.

## RENTAL DEDUCTIONS

**I understand there are limits on the deduction for payment of interest. I own four houses, of which two are rentals. How do interest deductions differ, and what are the limits?**

On your two nonrental houses, the deduction for the payment of mortgage interest is limited to loans of $1 million. The cost of interest on the other rentals is an expense deducted from rental income. But this expense also has certain limits, which depend on your adjusted gross income (AGI) and when you bought the rentals. If your rental income minus rental expenses produced a net loss, you can deduct up to $25,000 from your salary income if your AGI was below $100,000. Between $100,000 and $150,000 in AGI, that deduction is reduced by 50 percent of the amount exceeding $100,000. Above $150,000 AGI, losses are suspended, but you can use them to offset future rental income.

There is one exception: if you purchased the rentals before October 23, 1986, you can deduct 20 percent of your otherwise disallowed losses in 1989, 10 percent in 1990, and zero thereafter.

## SELLING YOUR HOME

**When I sell my home, do I have to pay taxes on the gain?**

You can defer taxes on the gain as long as you buy another home for the same price or more than the home you sold within two years. If the new home costs less, you can defer taxes on part of the gain. Additionally, if you are 55 or older, you may take advantage of a once-in-a-lifetime exemption from taxes on the first $125,000 in gain from the sale of your home. To qualify for this exemption, you must have owned and lived in the home for at least three of the five years preceding the sale.

## SELLING YOUR HOME AND BUYING A LESS EXPENSIVE HOME

**If I sell my house and purchase a less-expensive house, am I required to pay any taxes?**

Yes. You are required to pay taxes on the difference between the cost of the new residence and the adjusted sales price of the old home. The adjusted sales price of your old home equals the selling price of your old home less its cost basis and all costs to sell it. The cost basis is determined by adding to the price of the home all the costs you incurred in purchasing it plus the costs of improvements.

## TIME-SHARE DEDUCTIONS

**Besides my home, I own two time-share condominiums, which I'm entitled to use one week each year. How much of the interest is deductible on all three properties?**

You can deduct 100 percent of the interest on the loans used to buy your principal residence and one of the time-shares (considered a second home). Interest paid on the other time-share is considered personal interest, which is gradually being phased out. Personal interest is 20 percent deductible for 1989, 10 percent for 1990, and zero thereafter.

The time-share used for the second home must meet certain requirements. First, it must be used as security for the loan. Second, you actually have to own the property, even if for only one week of the year. This means that the way you take title to a time-share has a bearing on the qualification process. A "deeded" time-share qualifies; a "right-to-use" agreement does not.

## DEPRECIATING MOBILE HOMES

**Recently I moved out of my mobile home and have since begun renting it out. Can I depreciate it over 27.5 years as I could for a rental house?**

Yes, you can. Under the latest tax law, mobile homes are considered real property and can be depreciated over 27.5 years if a rental property. (The old tax laws considered mobile homes to be personal property and allowed depreciation over a 5- or 10-year period.)

# DEDUCTIBLE TAXES

**What taxes are deductible for purposes of federal income taxes?**

You can deduct state and local income taxes, personal property taxes, and real estate taxes. Sales taxes are *not* deductible.

# LOSS ON SALE OF RESIDENCE

**I sold my house for less than I paid for it. Is the loss deductible?**

Unfortunately, no. If you sell your principal residence for less than you paid for it, consider it lost money; it's not tax-deductible.

# TAX ADVANTAGES OF RENTAL UNIT

**My mother earns $32,000 annually and wants to purchase a fourplex. If she lives in one unit and manages the others as rentals, what tax benefits would she receive?**

Since your mother plans to reside in one of the four units, she can deduct one-quarter of the mortgage interest and real estate taxes. On the remaining three-fourths, she can take a business deduction for interest and taxes. She can also depreciate the rental portion over 27.5 years and deduct the costs of maintenance and utilities. Because she plans to manage the building actively, she can deduct from her salary income losses of up to $25,000 if the losses exceed any gains from other passive investments.

## WHEN TO BORROW

**Should I take out a mortgage now or wait until interest rates go lower?**

There is no telling exactly when interest rates will go up or down. As a rule, however, interest rates are either in a rising or falling trend; seldom are they stable. Once the initial direction changes, they will usually continue in that direction until a new trend develops. Therefore, if interest rates are rising, it would be an educated gamble that you would pay more for a loan if you waited. On the other hand, if rates were falling, it would be likely that you could get a cheaper rate if you waited. However, you should truly consider a loan on its merits. For example, ask yourself, "Is this the home I want to live in, and can I afford to borrow now to live in it, given the current interest rate? At today's rates can I make an acceptable profit on this investment property?" If rates then go up, you can pat yourself on the back for your timing. If rates go down a couple of points or more, you can always try to refinance. And even if rates fall later, the investment may still be the best one available *today*.

## FIXED-RATE OR ARM?

**Which type of loan is better—the fixed-rate or adjustable-rate mortgage?**

It essentially depends on how long you plan to keep the mortgage. Both types of loans have inherent advantages and disadvantages.

As a rule, if you plan to own the property four years or less, then the ARM will be more economical. If you own the property more than four years, then the fixed-rate mortgage will cost you less. This is primarily due to lower initial rates usually charged on an ARM, which in time gradually reach and surpass the rate of the fixed-rate mortgage.

Bear in mind that ARMs shift the risk of increasing interest rates from the lender to the borrower. In return, the borrower should get caps on the interest charged, as protection against drastically increasing rates. More important, the ARM is more likely than a fixed-rate mortgage to be assumable. Assumability is advantageous, because this added flexibility makes your property more marketable.

## SHOPPING FOR A LOAN

**Most institutional lenders seem to be very competitive. Are all their rates the same? If not, how much can I save by shopping around?**

Studies have shown that a homeowner can save up to $30,000 over the life of a mortgage if that person is an informed borrower. Rates can vary substantially among institutional lenders, and the educated borrower can save a surprising amount of money by making the correct decision. Like supermarkets, department stores, and other competing businesses, lenders charge different amounts for essentially the same thing. Lenders have different costs and desired profit margins. In addition, they attempt to establish different customer bases. Thus, lenders' offerings can differ in terms of rates and fees.

## INTEREST RATES ON BONDS

**I was told that the value of federal and municipal bonds goes down when interest rates go up. This doesn't seem logical to me. Would you clarify?**

What you were told is correct. Bond values rise when interest rates go down and, conversely, drop when interest rates go up. This is because the interest rate paid on the bonds is set when the bonds are issued. If rates go up, an existing bond is paying a lower rate than newly issued bonds, so it is worth less and its price falls. If rates fall, people can get a better return from the older bonds, so their price rises.

Let's say you buy an 8 percent municipal bond issued by the Township of Lansing; the bond has a face value of $5,000 and is due to mature in 2001. Until maturity you collect $400 a year in interest. At maturity you will be paid $5,000, unless Lansing defaults on its debt. After you buy that bond, Lansing Township issues more bonds on which it has to pay 10 percent interest because interest rates are higher than at the time your 8 percent bond was issued. Now, in the open marketplace, the value of the 8 percent bonds has dropped because an investor can buy 10 percent bonds for $5,000 and earn $500 a year. Why would an investor pay $5,000 for your bond when he or she can pay the same amount of money and earn 10 percent? So now your bond will sell for somewhat less than you paid for it. Of course, you can still hold on to your bond and collect $5,000 at maturity.

The inverse relationship between price and interest rate applies to all types of bonds, including corporate bonds issued by companies and United States Treasury securities issued by Uncle Sam.

# Glossary of Real Estate Terms

*Abandonment*  Voluntary relinquishment of rights of ownership or another form of interest (an easement) by failure to use the property over an extended period of time.

*Absentee landlord*  A lessor of real property (usually the owner) who does not reside on any portion of the property.

*Abstract of title*  A summary of the conveyances, transfers, and any other data relied on as evidence of title, together with any other elements of record that may impair the title. Still in use in some states, but giving way to the use of title insurance.

*Accelerated depreciation*  Depreciation occurring at a rate faster than equal amounts per year. This form of depreciation is usually used for special assets for income tax purposes.

*Acceleration clause*   A clause in a mortgage or trust deed giving the lender the right to call all monies owed to be immediately due and payable upon the happening of a certain stated event, such as sale of the property.

*Acceptance*   Agreement to abide by the terms of an offer.

*Access right*   A right to enter and exit one's property.

*Accretion*   Gradual deposit of soil from a waterway onto the adjoining land. The additional land generally becomes the property of the owner of the shore or bank, except where local statutes specify otherwise.

*Accrued depreciation*   The amount of depreciation accumulated over a period of time in the accounting process.

*Acknowledgment*   A formal declaration of execution of a document before an authorized official (usually a notary public) by a person who has executed (signed) a document.

*Acre*   A measure of land equal to 160 square rods (43,560 square feet). An acre is approximately 209 × 209 feet.

*Addendum*   Something added. A list or other items added to a document, letter, contract, escrow instructions, etc.

*Adjustable-rate mortgage (ARM)*   Mortgage with an interest rate that can change as often as specified in the loan agreement.

*Adjusted-cost basis*   The value of an asset on the accounting books of a taxpayer; the original cost plus improvements less depreciation.

*Adjusted sales price*   For income tax purposes, the selling price of a property less its acquisition cost and all the costs to sell it.

*Adjustment period*   A period of time from one rate change to another, usually one, three, or five years, in which the interest rate on an ARM is allowed to change. Thus, a mortgage with an adjustable period of one year is referred to as a one-year ARM.

*Adverse land use*   A use of land that causes the surrounding property to lose value, such as a truck terminal adjacent to a residential area.

*Adverse possession*   A method of acquiring title by open and notorious possession under an evident claim or right. Specific requirements for time of possession usually vary with each state.

*Affidavit*   A written statement or declaration sworn to or affirmed before some official who has the authority to administer affirmation. An oath.

*Agency agreement (listing)*   A listing agreement between the seller of real property and a broker wherein the broker's commission is protected against a sale by other agents but not by the principal (seller). Often referred to as a nonexclusive-agency listing.

*Agent*   A person authorized to represent or act for another in business matters.

*Agreement of sale*   A written contract between the buyer and the seller, where both parties are in full agreement on the terms and conditions of the sale.

*Alienation*   The transfer of property from one person to another.

*Alienation clause*   A clause within a loan instrument calling for a debt to be paid in its entirety upon the transfer of ownership of the secured property. Similar to a due-on-sale clause.

*All-inclusive trust deed (AITD)*   Same as wraparound mortgage, except with a deed of trust as the security instrument instead of a mortgage.

*Alluvion*   Soil deposited by accretion.

*Amenities*   Attractive or desirable features of a property, such as a swimming pool or view of the ocean.

*American Land Title Association (ALTA)*   A group of title insurance companies that issue title insurance to lenders.

*Amortization*   The liquidation of a financial obligation through equal payments in regular installments.

*Annuity*   (1) Cash payment over a given period. (2) A fixed amount given or left by will paid periodically.

*Appraisal*   An estimate and opinion of value; an objective conclusion resulting from an analysis of pertinent data.

*Appreciation*   Increase in value of property from improvements or the elimination of negative factors.

*Appurtenance*   Something belonging to the land and conveyed with it, such as buildings, fixtures, and rights.

*ARM*   Adjustable-rate mortgage.

*ASHI*   American Society of Home Inspectors.

*Assemblage*   Process of acquiring contiguous properties into one overall parcel for a specific use or to increase the value of the whole.

*Assessed value*    Value placed on property by the tax assessor.

*Assessment*    (1) The valuation of property for the purpose of levying a tax. (2) The amount of the tax levied.

*Assessor*    One appointed to assess property for taxation.

*Assigned mortgage*    A note that is transferred to another. For example, a note owed to you is an asset that someone is paying you interest on and that you can assign to another.

*Assignee*    One who receives an assignment.

*Assignment*    A transfer or making over to another the whole of any property, real or personal, or of any estate or right therein. To assign is to transfer.

*Assignor*    One who owns property assigned.

*Assumed mortgage*    The agreement of a buyer to assume the liability of an existing mortgage. Normally, the lender has to approve the new borrower before the existing borrower is released from the liability.

*Attachment*    Seizure of property by court order, usually in a pending lawsuit to make property available in case of judgment.

*Balance sheet*    A financial statement that shows the condition of a business or individual as of a particular date. Discloses assets, liabilities, and net worth.

*Balloon payment*    The final installment paid at the end of the term of a note; used only when preceding installments were not sufficient to pay off the note in full.

*Bankruptcy*   Procedure of federal law to seize the property of a debtor and divide the proceeds among the creditors.

*Base and meridian*   Imaginary lines used by surveyors to find and describe the location of public or private lands.

*Benchmark*   A mark used by surveyors that is permanently fixed in the ground to denote the height of that point in relation to sea level.

*Beneficiary*   The lender involved in a note and trust deed. One entitled to the benefit of a trust.

*Bequeath*   To give or leave personal property by a will.

*Bill of sale*   An instrument used to transfer personal property.

*Blanket mortgage (trust deed)*   A single mortgage (or trust deed) that covers more than one piece of real estate.

*Blighted area*   A declining area where property values are affected by destructive economic or natural forces.

*Blockbusting*   A method of informing a community of the fact that people of a different race or religion are moving into the neighborhood; this often causes property values to drop, thereby enabling homes to be obtained at below market value. Consequently, this practice is illegal.

*Board foot*   A unit of measuring lumber. One board foot is 12 × 12 × 1 inches, or 144 cubic inches.

*Bond*   (1) A method of financing debt by a government or corporation; the bond is interest-bearing and has priority over stock in terms of security. (2) An insurance agreement by which one party is insured against loss or default by another. In the construction business, a performance bond insures the interested party that the contractor will complete the project.

**Book value**    The value of an asset plus improvements less depreciation.

**Boot**    The additional value given when trading properties in order to equalize their values.

**Bottom land**    (1) Low-lying ground such as a valley. (2) Low land along a waterway formed by alluvial deposits.

**Breach**    Violation of an obligation in a contract.

**British thermal unit (Btu)**    The unit of heat required to raise one pound of water one degree Fahrenheit. Describes the capacity of heating and cooling systems.

**Broker (real estate)**    An agent licensed by the state to carry on the business of dealing in real estate. He or she usually receives a commission for services of bringing together buyers and sellers, or tenants and landlords.

**Building code**    A set of laws that control the design, materials, and similar factors in the construction of buildings.

**Building line**    A line set by law or deed a certain distance from the street line, in front of which an owner cannot build on a lot. Also known as a setback line.

**Built-ins**    Items that are not movable, such as stoves, ovens, built-in microwave ovens, and dishwashers.

*Built-up roof*   A form of level roof consisting of layers of roofing materials covered with fine gravel.

*Business opportunity*   The sale or lease of a business and goodwill (patronage and reputation) of an existing business enterprise.

*Buy option*   Lease with option to purchase.

*Buyers' market*   A market condition in which there are more sellers than interested buyers.

*Capital expenditures*   Money spent by a business on improvements such as land, building, and machinery.

*Capital gain*   For income tax purposes, the gain realized from the sale of an asset less the purchase price and deductible expenses.

*Capitalization*   An appraisal in which value is determined by considering net operating income and a reasonable percentage return on investment.

*Capitalization rate*   A percentage used to determine the value of income property through capitalization.

*Cash flow*   The owner's spendable income after deducting operating expenses and debt service.

*Caveat emptor*   A legal phrase meaning "let the buyer beware." The buyer takes the risk when purchasing an item without the protection of warranties.

*Certificate of Reasonable Value (CRV)*   An appraisal of real property issued by the Veterans Administration.

*Chain of title*   A history of conveyances and encumbrances affecting the title to real property as far back as records are available.

*Chattel*   Personal property.

*Chattel mortgage*  A mortgage on personal property, as distinguished from one on real property.

*Client*  One who employs another's services, such as those of an attorney, real estate agent, or insurance agent.

*Closing*  (1) In the sale of real estate, the final moment when all documents are executed and recorded and the sale is complete. (2) A general selling term describing the stage at which the buyer agrees to purchase.

*Closing costs*  Incidental expenses incurred with the sale of real property, such as appraisal fees, title insurance, and termite report.

*Closing statement*  A list of the final accounting of all monies of buyer and seller prepared by an escrow agent. It notes all costs each party must pay at the completion of a real estate transaction.

*Cloud on title*  An encumbrance on real property that affects the rights of the owner and that often keeps the title from being marketable until the cloud is removed.

*Collateral security*  A separate obligation attached to another contract pledging something of value to guarantee performance of the contract.

*Commercial bank*  An institution that offers checking accounts, loans, savings accounts, and services such as business loans. Banks are active in installment loans on vehicles and boats and construction financing, rather than in long-term real estate financing. *See also* Institutional lenders.

*Common area*  That area owned in common by owners of condominiums and planned unit development homes within a subdivision.

*Community property*   Real and personal property accumulated by a husband and wife during their marriage.

*Compound interest*   Interest paid on the original principal and on interest accrued.

*Condemnation*   A declaration by governing powers that a structure is unfit for use.

*Conditional sales contract*   A contract for the sale of property where the buyer has possession and use, but the seller retains title until the conditions of the contract have been fulfilled. Also known as a land contract or contract of sale.

*Condominium*   A system of ownership in a multi-unit structure where each living unit is individually owned but the unit owners jointly own the common areas and land.

*Conformity, principle of*   An appraisal term stating that uniformity throughout a certain area produces highest value.

*Conservator*   A court-appointed guardian.

*Consideration*   Anything of value given to induce someone to enter into a contract.

*Construction loan*   The short-term financing of improvements on real estate. Once the improvements are completed, a "take-out" loan for a longer term is used to pay off the existing construction loan.

*Contingency*   A condition upon which a valid contract depends. For example, the sale of a house may be contingent upon the buyer's obtaining adequate financing.

*Contract*   A written or oral agreement between two or more parties to do or not to do certain things.

*Contract of sale*    Conditional sales contract.

*Conventional loan*    A loan, usually on real estate, that is not backed by the federal agencies of FHA and VA.

*Convertible ARM*    An adjustable-rate mortgage that can convert to a fixed-rate mortgage.

*Conveyance*    The transfer of the title to land from one party to another.

*Cooperative apartment*    A building with two or more units in which the unit owners are required to purchase stock in the corporation that owns the property. The co-op was a forerunner of the condominium and is less popular because of the difficulty in financing, since the units are not individually owned.

*Corporation*    A legal entity having certain powers and duties of a natural person, together with rights and liabilities of both, distinct and apart from those persons composing it.

*Cost approach*    A method of appraisal whereby the estimated cost of a structure is calculated, less the land value and depreciation.

*Counteroffer*    An offer made in response to an offer. For example, *A* offers to buy *B*'s house for $80,000 although it is listed for $85,000. *B* makes a counteroffer to *A* by stating that she will sell the house to *A* for $81,000. The $81,000 offer is a counteroffer.

*Covenants*    Agreements written into deeds and other instruments stating performance or nonperformance of certain acts or noting certain uses or nonuses of the property.

*CPM*    Certified Property Manager.

*Cul de sac*   A dead-end street with a turnaround at the end.

*Current assets*   Assets that can readily be converted into cash, as with short-term accounts receivable and common stocks.

*Current liabilities*   Short-term debts.

*D.B.A. (Doing Business As)*   A business name or identification.

*Dedication*   The donation by an owner of private property for public use.

*Deed*   A written instrument that, when executed, conveys title of real property.

*Default*   Failure to fulfill or discharge an obligation or to perform any act that has been agreed to.

*Defendant*   The individual or entity against whom a civil or criminal action is brought.

*Deferred payments*   Payments to begin in the future.

*Deflation*   Opposite of inflation. The price of goods and services decrease in relation to the money available to buy them.

*Delivery*   The placing of property in the possession of the grantee.

*Demise*   A transfer of an estate by lease or will.

*Demographics*   Statistics about a population. Data used by certain businesses (especially chain stores), such as the traffic count regarding a possible new location.

*Density*   The amount of crowding together of buildings, people, or other given things.

*Depletion*    The reduction or loss in value of an asset.

*Deposit receipt*    The form used to accept an earnest-money deposit to secure the offer for the purchase of real property.

*Depreciation*    (1) For appraisal purpose, a loss of value of an asset brought about by age (positive deterioration) or functional and economic obsolescence. (2) For tax purposes, a percentage reduction of property value year by year.

*Depression*    That part of a business cycle where unemployment is high and production and overall purchasing by the public is low. A severe recession.

*Deterioration*    The gradual wearing away of a building from exposure to the elements. Also referred to as physical depreciation.

*Devise*    A gift of real estate by will.

*Diluvium*    A deposit of land left by a flood.

*Diminishing returns*    An economic condition in which an increase in capital or personnel does not increase production proportionately. (For example, whereas two laborers may do more than twice the work of one laborer, four laborers may do less than four times the work of one laborer.) The return diminishes when production is proportionately less than input.

*Directional growth*    The path of development of an urban area. Used to determine where future development will be most profitable.

*Divided interest*    Different interest in the same property, as in interests of the owner, lessee, or mortgagee.

*Documentary tax stamps*    Stamps affixed to a deed denoting the amount of transfer tax paid.

*Domicile*   The place where a person has a permanent home.

*Double-declining balance depreciation*   An accelerated method of depreciating an asset in which double the amount of straight-line depreciation is deducted from the remaining value of the asset each year.

*Dower*   The portion of her husband's estate that a wife inherits on his death in the absence of a will.

*Down payment*   Cash or other consideration paid toward a purchase by the buyer, as opposed to the amount that is financed.

*Due-on-sale clause*   A condition written into a financial instrument which gives the lender the right to require immediate repayment of the unpaid balance if the property is sold without consent of the lender.

*Earnest money*   That money deposited by the buyer in an offer to purchase real property in order to show good faith in completing the transaction.

*Easement*   A right or privilege with respect to real estate. An example is the legal right-of-way that permits an owner to cross another's land so as to get to his or her own property. An easement is appurtenant to the land, which means that it cannot be sold off separately and must be transferred with the title to the land of which it is part.

*Economic life*   The period over which property will yield a return on the investment.

*Economic obsolescence*   Loss of useful life and desirability of a property through economic forces, such as changes in zoning, changes in traffic flow, and so on, rather than deterioration.

*Economic rent*  The current market rental based on comparable rent for a similar unit.

*Effective age*  The age of a structure estimated by its condition as opposed to its actual age.

*Egress*  The right to go out across the land of another.

*Elevation*  (1) The height above sea level. (2) Architecturally, the view looking at the front of a structure.

*Emblements*  Crops growing on the land.

*Eminent domain*  The right of the government to acquire private property for public use by condemnation. The owner must be fully compensated.

*Encroachment*  Trespass. The building or any improvements partly or wholly on the property of another.

*Encumbrance*  Anything that affects or limits the fee simple title to property, such as mortgages, trust deeds, easements, or restrictions of any kind. Liens are special encumbrances that make the property security for the debt.

*Entity*  An existence or being, as in a corporation or business, rather than an individual person.

*Entrepreneur*  An independent businessperson taking risks for profit, as opposed to a salaried employee working for someone else.

*Equity*  (1) The value that an owner has in property over and above the liens against it. (2) In law, fairness rather than strict interpretation of the law.

*Equity buildup*  The reduction in the difference between property value and the amount of the lien as regular payments are made. The equity increases (builds up) on an amortized loan as the proportion of interest payment gets smaller, causing the amount going toward principal to increase.

*Equity participation*    Equity sharing.

*Equity partnership*    Equity sharing.

*Equity sharing*    Shared ownership of real property. Also known as shared equity, equity participation, equity partnership, and shared appreciation.

*Escalation clause*    A clause in a lease providing for an increase in rent at a future time because of increased costs to the lessor, as in cost-of-living index, tax increases, and so on.

*Escheat*    The reverting of property to the state in the absence of heirs.

*Escrow*    A neutral third party who carries out the provisions of an agreement.

*Estate*    (1) An ownership interest in real property. (2) A large home with spacious grounds. (3) A deceased person's property.

*Estate for years*    Any estate for a specific period of time. A lease.

*Exclusive-right-to-sell listing*    A written contract between agent and owner in which the agent has the right to collect a commission if the listed property is sold by anyone during the term of the agreement.

*Executor*    The person appointed in a will to carry out the terms of the will.

*Face value*    The value stated on the face of notes, mortgages, and so on, without consideration of any discounting.

*Fair market value*   The price a property will bring, given that buyer and seller are fully aware of market conditions and comparable properties.

*Feasibility survey*   A study of an area before development of a project in order to predict whether the project will succeed.

*Fed*   Nickname for the Federal Reserve System.

*Federal Deposit Insurance Corporation (FDIC)*   The federal corporation that insures depositors against loss up to a specified amount, currently $100,000. The FDIC's Bank Insurance Fund (BIF) covers bank deposits, and its Savings Association Insurance Fund (SAIF) covers deposits in savings and loan associations.

*Federal Home Loan Banks*   A system of regional banks that banks, savings and loan associations, insurance companies, and similar institutions may join to borrow money to use in making available home financing. Its purpose is to make a permanent supply of financing available for home loans.

*Federal Home Loan Mortgage Corporation (FHLMC) (Freddie Mac)*   A federal agency that purchases first mortgages from members of the Federal Reserve System and the Federal Home Loan Bank System.

*Federal Housing Administration (FHA)*   The federal agency that insures first mortgages on homes (and other projects), enabling lenders to extend more lenient terms to borrowers who qualify.

*Federal National Mortgage Association (FNMA) (Fannie Mae)*   A private corporation that purchases first mortgages at discounts.

*Federal Reserve System*   A government agency, commonly referred to as the Fed, which consists of a 12-

member Federal Open Market Committee, 12 Fed branches, and approximately 6,000 member banks. Its primary purpose is to control the supply of money.

*Fee simple*   Ownership of real property without any limitation, so that it can be sold, left at will, or inherited.

*Fiduciary*   A person in a position of trust and confidence, as between principal and broker. The broker as a fiduciary owes loyalty and other duties to the principal.

*First mortgage*   A mortgage having priority over all other voluntary liens against a specific property.

*Fixed-rate mortgage*   A mortgage loan wherein the rate of interest charged the borrower remains constant over the loan term.

*Fixtures*   Items, such as plumbing and electrical fixtures, affixed to buildings or land, usually in such a way that they cannot be removed without damage to themselves or the property.

*Foreclosure*   Procedure in which property pledged as security for a debt is sold at public auction to pay the debt after a default in payment and terms.

*Free and clear*   Subject to no liens, especially voluntary liens.

*Front footage*   (1) The linear measurement along the front of a parcel of land. (2) The portion of the parcel that fronts the street or walkway.

*Functional obsolescence*   Loss in value attributable to out-of-date or poorly designed equipment where newer equipment and structures have been invented.

*Government National Mortgage Association (GNMA) (Ginnie Mae)*     Federal agency that purchases first mortgages at discounts, in a role similar to that of FNMA.

*Graduated lease*     A lease that provides for rental adjustments, often based upon future determination of the cost-of-living index. Used for the most part in long-term leases.

*Graduated payment mortgage (GPM)*     A mortgage with payments that increase over its term.

*Grant*     A transfer of interest in real property, such as an easement.

*Grantee*     One to whom a grant is made.

*Grantor*     One who grants a property or its rights.

*Gross income*     Total scheduled income from property before deducting any expenses.

*Gross-income multiplier*     A general appraising rule of thumb that, when multiplied by the gross annual income of a property, will estimate the market value. For example, the property sells for 7.2 times the gross income.

*Gross lease*     A lease obligating the lessor to pay all or part of the expenses incurred on a leased property.

*Ground lease*     A lease of vacant land.

*Ground rent*     Rent paid for vacant land.

*Growing-equity mortgage (GEM)*     A mortgage with payments that increase over a specified term. Increases are applied directly to principal reduction.

*Hardwood*     Wood, such as oak, maple, and walnut, used for interior finish, as opposed to soft woods.

*Highest and best use*    In appraisal, the use of land that will bring the highest economic return over a given time.

*Homeowners' association*    (1) An association of condominium owners, who vote on decisions regarding the complex and pay dues. (2) An association of homeowners within a community formed to improve and maintain the quality of the community.

*Homestead*    A declaration by the owner of a home that protects the home against judgments up to specified amounts provided by certain state laws.

*Hypothecate*    To give a thing as security without giving up possession of it, as with mortgaging real property.

*Impound account*    A trust account held for the purpose of paying taxes, insurance, and other periodic expenses incurred with real property.

*Improved real estate*    Land that has been built upon.

*Improvements*    Buildings, roads, and utilities that have been added to raw (unimproved) land.

*Inflation*    An increase in the supply of money, causing prices to rise.

*Installment note*    A note that provides for regular monthly payments to be made on the date specified in the instrument.

*Installment sale*    Sale of property in which the seller accepts a note for part or all of the price.

*Institutional lenders*    Banks, savings and loan associations, or other businesses that make loans to the public during their ordinary course of business, as opposed to individuals who fund loans.

*Instrument*    A written legal document.

*Intangible value*    The value of the goodwill or well-advertised name of an established business.

*Interest*    (1) Money charged for the use of money (principal). (2) A share or right in some property.

*Interest rate caps*    Limits in the amount of increases in the interest rate itself. Caps come in two varieties: they can limit the amount of increase in rate of interest charged from one adjustment period to the next; or they can limit the amount of increase over the life of the loan.

*Interim loan*    A short-term loan usually for real estate improvements during the period of construction.

*Intestate*    The condition of dying without having made a will.

*Intrinsic value*    The value of a thing by itself without certain aspects that will add value to some and not to others, as with a vintage Rolls Royce, which might have value to a car collector but to few others.

*Investment*    The laying out of money in the purchase of some form of property intending to earn a profit.

*Involuntary lien*    A lien that attaches to property without consent of the owner, such as tax liens, as opposed to voluntary liens (such as a mortgage).

*Joint tenancy*    Joint ownership by two or more persons with right of survivorship. Upon the death of a joint tenant, the interest does not go to the heirs but to the remaining joint tenants.

*Junior mortgage*    A mortgage lower in priority than a first mortgage; a second or third mortgage.

*Land contract*    Conditional sales contract.

*Land grant*    A gift of public land by the federal government.

*Landlord*    The owner of rented property.

*Lease*    A contract between the owner of real property (lessor) and another person (lessee) covering the conditions by which the lessee may occupy and use the property.

*Lease with option to purchase*    A lease that gives the lessee the option to purchase the leased property according to terms set forth in the contract.

*Legacy*    A gift of personal property by will.

*Legal description*    The geographical identification of a parcel of land.

*Legatee*    One who receives personal property from a will.

*Lessee*    One who contracts to rent property under a lease.

*Lessor*    An owner who enters into a lease with a tenant (lessee).

*Leverage*    The use of a small amount of cash to control a much greater value of assets.

*Liability*    A debt or obligation.

*Lien*    An encumbrance against real property for money, as in taxes, mortgages, and judgments.

*Life estate*    An estate in real property for the life of a person.

*Limited partnership*    A partnership of one or more general partners, who operate a business, along with one or more limited partners, who contribute capital. This arrangement restricts the limited partners' liability to the amount of money they contributed.

*Liquidate*    Dispose of property or assets or settle debts.

*Liquidity*    The degree to which an asset is readily convertible into cash.

*Lis pendens*    A recorded legal notice showing pending litigation of real property. Anyone acquiring an interest in such property after the recording of *lis pendens* could be bound to the outcome of the litigation.

*Listing*    A contract between owner and broker to sell the owner's real property.

*Loan broker*    Mortgage broker.

*Loan-to-value ratio (LTVR)*    The ratio, expressed as a percentage, of the amount of a loan to the value of real property.

*Long-term capital gain*    The gain incurred on the sale of an asset held for at least six months.

*MAI (Member, Appraisal Institute)*    A designation issued to a member of the American Institute of Real Estate Appraisers who has met specific qualifications.

*Maintenance reserve*    Money held in reserve to cover anticipated maintenance expenses.

*Margin*    For lending purposes, that amount added to a certain index rate, which results in the interest rate charged the borrower.

*Marketable title*    A salable title free of objectionable liens or encumbrances.

*Market-data approach*   An appraisal method to determine value by comparing similar properties to the subject property.

*Market value*   The price a buyer will pay and a seller will accept, both being fully informed of market conditions.

*Master plan*   A comprehensive zoning plan to allow a city to grow in an orderly manner.

*Mechanic's lien*   A lien created by statute on a specific property for labor or materials contributed to an improvement on that property.

*Metes and bounds*   A legal description used in describing boundary lines.

*Mineral rights*   Ownership of the minerals beneath the ground. The owner of mineral rights doesn't necessarily own the surface land.

*Moratorium*   Temporary suspension of the enforcement of liability for a debt.

*Mortgage*   An instrument by which property is hypothecated to secure the payment of a debt.

*Mortgage broker*   A person who, for a fee, brings together a lender with a borrower. Also known as a loan broker.

*Mortgage contract*   Security for the debt owed in a mortgage document.

*Mortgagee*   One who lends the money and receives the mortgage.

*Mortgage Guaranty Insurance Corporation (MGIC)*   Private corporation that insures mortgage loans.

*Mortgage note*   Evidence of the debt in a mortgage document.

*Mortgagor*   One who borrows on a property and gives a mortgage as security.

*Multiple-listing service (MLS)*   An organization of brokers in which a listing taken by one broker is circulated among all members, who have an opportunity to find a buyer.

*Negative amortization*   The opposite of amortization, which means paying off a loan over a period of time. Under negative amortization, the borrower will actually owe more than was borrowed.

*Net income*   Gross income less operating expenses.

*Net lease*   A lease requiring the tenant to pay all or part of the expenses on leased property in addition to the stipulated rent.

*Net listing*   A listing whereby an agent may retain as compensation all sums received over and above a net price to the owner. Illegal in some states.

*Net worth*   Total assets and liabilities of an individual, corporation, or business.

*Nonexclusive listing*   A listing in which the agent has an exclusive listing with respect to other agents; however, the owner may sell the property without being liable for a commission.

*Notary public*   One who is authorized by federal or local government to attest authentic signatures and administer oaths.

*Note*   A written instrument acknowledging a debt and promising payment.

*Notice to quit*    A notice issued by landlord to the tenant to vacate rented property, usually for nonpayment of rent or breach of contract.

*Offer*    A presentation to form a contract or agreement.

*One-year ARM*    An adjustable-rate mortgage in which the interest rate is allowed to change every year.

*Open listing*    An authorization given by an owner to a real estate agent to sell the owner's property. Open listings may be given to more than one agent without liability, and only the one who secures a buyer on satisfactory terms gets paid a commission.

*Operating expenses*    Expenses relevant to income-producing property, such as taxes, management, utilities, insurance, and other day-to-day costs.

*Option*    A right given, for consideration, to purchase or lease property upon stipulated terms within a specific period of time.

*Passive activity*    Any activity that involves the conduct of any trade or business in which the taxpayer does not materially participate. Any rental activity is a passive activity even if the taxpayer materially participates. Tax deductibility of losses from a passive activity is limited.

*Payment caps*    Specified limits of an ARM on how much the monthly payment can increase in any adjustment period or over the term of the loan.

*Percentage lease*    A lease on property in which normally a minimum specified rent is paid or a percentage of gross receipts of the lessee is paid, whichever is higher.

*Personal property*   Property that is not real property.

*Planned unit development*   Five or more individually owned lots where one or more other parcels are owned in common or there are reciprocal rights in one or more other parcels; subdivision.

*Plat book*   A book containing plat maps of a certain area.

*Plat map*   A map or plan of a specified parcel of land.

*Point*   (1) One percent. (2) A one-point fee often charged by the lender to originate the loan. On FHA and VA loans, the seller pays points to accommodate the loan.

*Power of attorney*   An instrument authorizing a person to act as the agent of the person granting the power.

*Preliminary title report*   The report of condition of the title before a sale or loan transaction. Once it is completed, a title insurance policy is issued.

*Prepayment penalty*   A penalty within a note, mortgage, or trust deed imposing a penalty if the debt is paid in full before the end of its term.

*Prime lending rate*   The interest rate charged by an institutional lender to its best customers.

*Principal*   (1) The amount of debt or investment, not including interest. (2) The employer of an agent.

*Private mortgage insurance (PMI)*   Insurance on a portion of the first mortgage allowing the lender to offer more lenient terms to a borrower.

*Progression*    Principle that the worth of an inferior property will tend to approach that of more expensive properties surrounding it.

*Proration of taxes*    Division of taxes equally or proportionately to time of use.

*Purchase agreement*    An agreement between buyer and seller denoting price and terms of the sale.

*Purchase-money mortgage*    A mortgage given by the buyer to the seller as part of the purchase consideration.

*Pyramid*    To build an estate by multiple acquisitions of properties using the initial properties as a base for further investment.

*Quitclaim deed*    A deed used to remove clouds on a title by relinquishing any right, title, or interest that the grantor may have.

*Real estate investment trust (REIT)*    A method of group investment with certain tax advantages. It is governed by federal and state laws.

*Real property*    Land and generally anything erected on, growing on, or attached to the land.

*Realtor*    A real estate broker holding membership in a real estate board affiliated with the National Association of Realtors.

*Redemption*    (1) The buying back of one's property after it has been lost through foreclosure. (2) Payment of delinquent taxes after sale to the state.

*Regression*    Principle that a higher value property will tend to fall to that of the lesser-quality properties surrounding it.

*Rent*  Consideration, usually money, for the occupancy and use of real property.

*Replacement-cost method*  A method of appraisal that determines value by computing the cost to make an exact replica.

*Request for notice of default*  A request by a lender that is recorded for notification in the case of default by a loan with priority.

*Reverse annuity mortgage (RAM)*  A mortgage in which the borrower is paid an annuity (income) drawn against the equity in the home.

*Right of survivorship*  Right to acquire the interest of a decreased joint owner. Distinguishing characteristic of joint tenancy.

*Right-of-way*  A privilege given by the owner of a property to give another the right to pass over private land.

*Riparian rights*  The right of a landowner to water on, under, or adjacent to the land owned.

*Sale-leaseback*  A sale and subsequent lease of the same property from the buyer back to the seller.

*Savings and loan association*  An institution that retains deposits for savers and lends out these deposits primarily for home loans.

*Secondary financing*  A junior loan or a loan second in priority to a first mortgage or trust deed.

*Security deposit*  Money given to a landlord by the tenant to secure performance of the rental agreement.

*Sellers' market*  A time when there are more buyers than sellers.

*Separate property*  Property owned by husband or wife that is not community property. Property acquired before marriage or by a gift, will, or inheritance.

*Setback line*  Building line.

*Severalty*  An estate held by one person alone, an individual right. The term is misleading, as it does not mean several persons own the property. Distinguished from joint tenancy.

*Shared appreciation*  Equity sharing.

*Shared appreciation mortgage (SAM)*  A mortgage that allows the lender to share in the appreciation of the property in return for a lower rate of interest.

*Sheriff's deed*  Deed given by court order in connection with the sale of a property to satisfy a judgment.

*Single-family residence*  A house as distinguished from an apartment house, a condominium, or a planned unit development.

*Special assessment*  Legal charge against real estate by a public authority to pay the cost of public improvements (for example, sewers) by which the property is benefited.

*Speculator*  One who buys property with the intent of selling it quickly at a profit.

*Straight-line depreciation*  Reducing value for tax purposes over a predetermined period of time by equal increments.

*Straight note*  A nonamortized note promising to repay a loan, signed by the debtor and including the amount, date due, and interest rate.

*Subdivision*   A division of one parcel of land into smaller lots.

*Subject to mortgage*   A condition of taking title in which the buyer is not responsible to the holder of the note. The original maker of the note is not released from the liability of the note, and the most the new buyer can lose in foreclosure is equity in the property.

*Sublease*   A lease given by a lessee.

*Syndicate*   A group of investors who invest in one or more properties through a partnership, corporation, or trust.

*Take-out commitment*   Agreement by a lender to have available a long-term loan over a specified time once construction is completed.

*Tax base*   The assessed value multiplied by the tax rate to determine the amount of tax due.

*Tax sale*   A sale of property, usually at auction, for nonpayment of taxes assessed against it.

*Tenancy in common*   Ownership by two or more persons who hold an undivided interest without right of survivorship.

*Tenant*   The holder of real property under a rental agreement. Also referred to as a lessee.

*Tender*   An offer of money, usually in satisfaction of a claim or demand.

*Tenements*   (1) All rights in land that pass with the conveyance of the land. (2) Certain groups of multiple dwellings.

*Testator*   A person who leaves a legally valid will at death.

*Tight money*   A condition in the money market in which demand for the use of money exceeds the available supply.

*Time-share*   Shared ownership wherein the owners are allowed limited use of a property.

*Title insurance*   Insurance written by a title company to protect the property owner against loss, if title is imperfect.

*Topography*   Character of the surface of land. Topography may be level, rolling, or mountainous.

*Township*   A territorial subdivision six miles long, six miles wide, and containing 36 sections, each one mile square.

*Tract house*   A house similar to other homes within a subdivision and built by the same developer, as opposed to a custom home built to owner specifications.

*Trade fixtures*   Personal property of a business that is attached to the property but can be removed upon the sale of the property.

*Trust deed*   An instrument that conveys legal title of a property to a trustee to be held pending fulfillment of an obligation, usually the repayment of a loan to a beneficiary (lender).

*Trustee*   One who holds bare legal title to a property in trust for another to secure performance of a debt obligation.

*Trustor*   The borrower of money secured by a trust deed.

*Unimproved land*   Land in its natural state without structures on it.

*Unlawful detainer*   An action of law to evict a person or persons illegally occupying real property.

*Usury*   Interest rate charged on a loan in excess of that permitted by law.

*Variable interest rate*   A fluctuating interest rate that can go up or down depending on the market rate.

*Vendee*   A purchaser or buyer.

*Vendor*   A seller.

*Vested*   Bestowed upon someone or secured by someone, as with title to property.

*Voluntary lien*   A lien such as a mortgage, that attaches with the consent of the owner, as opposed to an involuntary lien (for example, taxes).

*Waive*   To relinquish or abandon; to forgo a right to enforce or require something.

*Wraparound mortgage*   A second mortgage that is subordinate to but includes the face value of the first mortgage. Also referred to as an all-inclusive trust deed.

*Yield*   Ratio, expressed as a percentage, of income from an investment to the total cost of the investment over a given period of time.

*Zoning*   Act of city or county authorities specifying how property may be used in specific areas.